Real
Wrexham

Real
Wrexham

Grahame Davies

Series Editor: Peter Finch

seren

Seren is the book imprint of
Poetry Wales Press Ltd
Nolton Street, Bridgend, Wales
www.seren-books.com

ISBN 978-1-85411-449-5

A CIP record for this title is available from
the British Library

The publisher works with the financial assistance
of the Welsh Books Council

Printed by Bell & Bain Ltd, Glasgow

Mixed Sources
Product group from well-managed
forests and other controlled sources
www.fsc.org   Cert no. TT-COC-002769
© 1996 Forest Stewardship Council

CONTENTS

PREFACE

Wrexham, so good they named it twice. Wrexham Abbot, owned by
the abbeys, and Wrexham Regis with its allegiance to the Crown.
The boundary between these ancient townships can still be traced.
It spirals in from the River Clywedog in Erddig Park to track the railway into Wrexham Central. It then rolls along the middle of Abbot
Street, High Street, Yorke Street, and Tuttle Street before turning
back on itself, through the Coed y Glyn estate, to meet the Clywedog
once more. As disparate conurbations representing God and King,
Abbot and Regis have faced each other for so long now that the dif-
ferences between them have evaporated. Protestants and Catholics
in Northern Ireland undistinguished by surname; Palestinians and
Jews without yarmulke and kufi; Cardiff and Swansea minus
Burberry and Cyril the Swan.

Wrexham, population 42,576, is now the largest town in Wales. In
the clamour for status it lost out to Newport, three times larger, in the
last round of city creation in 2002. Before that, in 1998, it had offered
itself and the splendour of north-east Wales as home for the new
National Assembly. Lost out there as well. Wrexham today is an independent-minded conurbation of Welsh dimension. No visible cultural
overload. There's an art centre and a little theatre, one too many
branches of Poundstretcher and its clones maybe, but a total lack of
pretension. The B-level students from the local Technical, Art and
Tertiary Colleges fill the centre with goths, emos and skaters. There
are small town boom-box boy racers and a bus station unpolluted by
porno merchants. You can walk here.

Over the years I've visited this place many times. And mostly I
found it a place too small for sophistication, too big to be beautiful,
and with smoke from the nineteenth century still in the air. But today,
in the new millennium, with early sunshine filling the pedestrianised
streets, I find a clean town, of easy proportion, with a scattering of
fine Victorian and Georgian buildings still extant among the branches
of Wallis, Next and Burton.

Wrexham Central with its hourly diesels to Liverpool could be in
the running for the shortest station in Wales award. The stubby platform is in Regis but the track in Abbot. Where it used to run to in the
grand days is now a shopping mall, kids in white tracksuits wearing ear
buds, women with shopping trolleys, men with boxes and plastic bags:
JD, Holland and Barrett, HMV, car park, plantings, indistinguishable

from retail parks the world over. Even the Brewery that made the town famous for its lager has been demolished to make way for the Central Retail Park. All that remains is the original office and tun house from 1882. Empty when I visit, with the graffiti THIS SHOULD BE A PUB encouragingly scrawled outside.

But not all of Wrexham is like this. The central streets are narrow and beautifully car free. They have irregular rooflines, Georgian porchways, Victorian arcades and a timber-framed pub, in Hope Street, right in the centre. The Horse & Jockey is still thatched, and still serving local beers. Wrexham could be a town of Inns. The vast and vertical drinkeries have yet to arrive. User-scale pubs dot the townscape. The Walnut Tree, Seven Stars, The Old Vaults, The One To Five, The Elihu Yale.

Elihu Yale, famous Wrexham son, is worth tracking. How do you get to be called that? 'Elihu' is Biblical. He was descendant of Abraham and antagonist of Job. 'Yale' is an Anglicisation of Iâl. Yale's family came from Plas yn Iâl in Denbighshire. He made his money in India and then spent some of it founding the great American University named after him in New Haven, Connecticut. He is buried in the yard at St Giles' Church. The 135-foot church tower, one of the seven wonders of Wales, is replicated at half size in America. Yale's grave is marked with a monument of his own devising. "Much good, some ill, he did; so hope's all even", runs the inscription in an eighteenth century serifed font.

Inside I am accosted by an ancient in a knitted cap who could have walked here straight from Dibley. Are you an engineer? God, do I look like one? Over the arch of the east wall is the famous early sixteenth century *Doom Painting*[1] put there to show the ignorant just what would happen when the trumpet of judgement sounded. Cartoon figures emerge from their coffins to rise towards God, fear in their sunken eyes, decay evident in their bloodless limbs. On the north side is a white marble memorial showing a woman also rising from her coffin.[2] Death might elsewhere be dark and still but here in St Giles they are determined to offer luminous hope. That's Mary Myddleton. The money her family made was used to make cannons. Famous for it. War and God, marching side by side.

Wrexham is not multi-ethnic to any significant degree. Few enrobed with djellaba, hijab, or burka. Nothing like Swansea or Cardiff although the arrival of refugee Iraqi Kurds at the tough Caia Park Estate,[3] dispersed there by over-zealous New Labour, did spark days of rioting in 2003. Hot summer nights and alcohol, claimed the media. In reality more to do with the pains of an impoverished and rarely represented white underclass. The Kurds moved on, some of them. But today Wrexham is the Polish capital in exile. Political parties print their election leaflets in Polish. There are Polish newspapers, day centres, shops and clubs. On the streets in 2007 you can hear as much Polish as Welsh, both mixing with an English whose accent owes more to Cheshire than Denbigh or Meirionnydd.

The Town Museum was built to celebrate the Borough Council rather than ancient Abbot or Regis. Here, amid the displays of mayoral regalia, assemblages of embossed red Wrexham brick, and enlarged and grainy photographs showing how the world used to be before colour was invented, is 'Brymbo Man'. A beaker burial discovered in 1958 by Ron Pritchard, pipe trench digger, outside 79 Cheshire View, Brymbo. Work stopped as the three and a half thousand year old bones, the cracked pottery beaker and the skull itself were recovered from the ditch. He's there now, in his museum case, lying on a bed of sand. In 1998 when he travelled back here from his period of sombre analysis at the National Museum of Wales at in Cardiff he did the trip in a hearse. Manchester University's Dr Caroline Wilkinson has made a face reconstruction. How he must have looked. Head in a glass case, lit by low light. I wanted him to resemble Grahame Davies but he looks more like Mick Hucknall, rosy Irish cheeks, 70s rock band hair, the frown you'd expect on a man with no body. That's unreconstructed, as yet.

At the library I hunt out the café made famous by Aled Lewis Evans in his Welsh novel[4] of old ladies, cream cakes and the mystic young who frequent such places Wales over. There's a seventy year-old reading the contents of his wallet, a pair of students encumbered by bags and files, a child eating an egg sandwich and two pairs of female pensioners eating scones. Attire by M&S. Primary colour – blue. On the window in white Times 30-point is an unattributed text: "He is selling his flat to go to Brazil. There he learns Portuguese by reading *Folha de S. Paulo* in the café for hours and hours. He reads the newspaper with his dictionary in his hands. He meets his future wife. Six months later they come to the UK to meet his parents." I ask a middle-aged couple in blue anoraks if they know what it means. They don't. "Art", says the woman. They nod their heads.

Near here, according to an exhibition in the Art Centre foyer (seventy votes already cast, huge local interest), Landmark Wales will build a sculpture to mark the gateway to Wrexham. In contention are a blue and white tower, twin hands, one in red the other in white, a castle that might be made from gravestones, a wreck of ornamental cast metal and a box of letterforms masquerading as dragon bones. My money is on the letters, which mix *Wales* with *Cymru*. A concrete poem for the age of the soundbite. Literature for the illiterate. Words for those who usually never bother. A Welsh marker for one of the northern beginnings of Wales. The chosen site is the A483 and A5 junction in nearby Chirk. If the project is a success it will be the sign-board for burgeoning Wrexham. If the gods fail it then it will be something they've built in Chirk. Watch it as you drive past.

I've walked in a great Abbot circle, the older town. In 1857, when there were only 646 registered voters, the whites took on the reds and the reds won. The whites were the Liberals and the reds the Tories. Corruption was easy and rife. You only had a few hundred pockets to line. Today almost everyone can vote but most don't bother. John Marek, now defeated independent Wrexham Assembly Member, has his HQ in a poster-plastered end of terrace near the football ground. His urgings to keep him in power mix with those of Safeway Scaffold and the men there to fix his roof. He was beaten by Lesley Griffiths in 2007. Politics remains a volatile game.

Grahame Davies' book takes the 'real' idea developed in my *Real Cardiff* volumes and applies it brilliantly to greater Wrexham. Describe the topography, track the history, look down alleys and under stones, find out where the past went, and who was once famous here and who is famous now, tell us how you fit in and then just what it is that this place means. Avoid the obvious. Make it real. *Real Wrexham* is the magnificent result.

Peter Finch
Cardiff, June 2007

notes

1. Vast early sixteenth century wall painting of *The Day of Judgement*, re-discovered after being painted over in 1867.
2. Memorial by Louis François Roubiliac to *Mary Myddleton* (1688-1747) of Croesnewydd Hall, Wrexham.
3. Population 11,000 with a high incidence of single white males. The Kurds were given hard-to-let flats in some of the estate's toughest corners.
4. *Y Caffi*, (Gwasg Pantycelyn), 2002. The author claims the book to be not explicitly based on the café at Wrexham although his useful groundplan on page 10 seems to be an exact replica.

INTRODUCTION

This is a border town. A place where mountain meets plain, where sheep-bitten moor meets lowland dairy pasture, where stone meets brick, and where people, accents and languages meet, mingle and merge. This is Wales' Eastern Front, the place where the tide of English conquest raced in, hit the mountain wall, faltered, and stopped, and where a 1200-year-old earthwork, Offa's Dyke, shows the invaders' high water mark.

The town itself occupies a platform between the brown buttresses of the Berwyn mountains to the west and the green expanses of the Cheshire Plain to the east. Not for nothing did the medieval Welsh call the place 'Caer Fantell', the Mantle Fortress. It was spread out in front of the strongholds of the hills like a matador's cape, a challenge to all comers. By then, in the middle ages, this had been Celtic territory for a couple of millennia. The Romans had come, put up a few small forts, mined the lead at Minera, set up a pottery works at Holt, and, by the end of the fourth century, had gone, leaving only a few pots, coins and brooches for future archaeologists. As they went, the pagan Angles and Saxons came, finding lowland Britannia soft and prosperous after hundreds of years of Roman rule, and virtually undefended now the legions had gone. In a couple of centuries, the territory was under new management, and rebranded: England.

But the takeover only went so far – as far as the foothills of the Cambrian mountains to the west, where the remaining Britons had made their stand and were now calling themselves the 'Cymry', the compatriates. For their part, the Saxons called them 'foreigners', '*wealas*', Welsh. The terms were as mutually exclusive as mountain and plain. Geographically, militarily, culturally, politically, it was an *impasse*. And once Offa built his dyke in the late eighth century, the demarcation was set in the landscape like scar tissue, forever.

The dyke was built to the west of where Wrexham stands today. But in the changing seasons of border warfare, the Welsh frontier was soon re-established far to the east of it, along the River Dee. Looking at the geography of the Wrexham area today – most of it is lowland, lacking natural defences – it seems extraordinary that the place should have remained Welsh for so long. True, it changed hands a few times after the Saxons arrived, but it was back in native control, albeit precariously, in the late thirteenth century, when Edward I of England launched his final campaign to conquer his infuriatingly independent western neighbour.

The key to why this exposed salient retained its freedom so long was not in the sharpness of its contours. It was in the depth of its forests. The lowlands of Maelor were cloaked by a dense tree cover extending for miles in every direction. In the tangled undergrowth, the invaders' weight of numbers counted for little, and the less numerous defenders could fight on something like equal odds, a Celtic Viet Cong. The guerrilla tactics of the Welsh archers made sure that any military expedition by the medieval superpower into the darkness of the forest was very costly indeed. Edward's solution, finally, was to use the medieval equivalent of Agent Orange: hundreds of woodcutters from all over England, who hacked down the forests for a bowshot's length on either side, so his juggernaut of conquest could roll in.

And roll in it did, in 1282, when the independence of the Welsh princes was at last extinguished with the death of Llywelyn ap Gruffudd. Edward himself stopped in Wrexham on his way to his final victory, sending off a couple of business letters as he did so.[1] After the conquest, the lands were duly parcelled out to his supporters. It seemed as though the matter was settled. And politically, and militarily, it was.

But culturally, and geographically, it wasn't. Political rulers come and go. People and memories are more enduring. In 2007, the British government, concerned about getting new immigrants to integrate in British society, published a guide for those who want to become naturalised: *Life in the United Kingdom: A Journey to Citizenship*. Referring to Wales, it mentions Edward's conquest, and then adds, either with weariness or grudging respect, that language and culture are remarkably resistant to political changes. It's true. More than seven centuries after the conquest, the placenames still clog with Celtic consonants the moment you cross the river Dee, gradients steepen, black-and-white half-timber gives way to grey stone, grass becomes gorse, accents, like the landscape, lose their flatness and start to dip and climb. It's subtle. Shaded, not sudden. But in a short while, you find the change has become unmistakable.

Over the years, the Wrexham area has been a palette of different influences. The name of the town itself is of uncertain origin. It's first mentioned in the twelfth century, and in varying spellings: Wristlesham, Wrettesham, Wrechcessam, Wrightlesham, Wryxham and Wrixham, and with Gwrexham and Gwregsam as Welsh alternatives. Apart from the 'ham' suffix, a Saxon word meaning a settlement, no-one is certain what the name means.[2] Which is fitting for a place with such a mixed heritage. It's been fought over by Welsh defenders and Norman invaders, and disputed by Royalists and Parliamentarians; its lands have been enclosed by landowners, gutted by mining, piled with steelworks slag, and covered with acres of red-brick terraces, commuter homes, industrial estates and retail parks. Does it feel Welsh? Not like Dolgellau or Blaenau Ffestiniog away to the west, no. It's not a slate-grey Shangri Lla hiding from outsiders in the high mountains. Does it feel English? No, not like aristocratic Chester, its patrician neighbour, where even the shops are too grand to have entrances on the ground-floor. So does that mean Wrexham lacks identity? Again, no. It knows exactly what it is: a place where landscapes, economies and cultures converge. A place of encounter and transition. A place where one and one make three. A border town.

notes

1. Commanding that Valle Crucis Abbey at Llangollen be spared. A.H.Dodd, *A History of Wrexham*, (WBC, 1989), p18.
2. *Ibid*, p14. See also John Jones, *Wrexham and its Neighbourhood* (Wrexham, 1859),v. His brief introduction is disarmingly frank about the town:"It has no history relative or individual."

CENTRAL

The clearest way to experience the change from England to Wales in Wrexham is to head west along the new A483 bypass from Chester to Wrexham. It runs straight as an invader's arrow across the Cheshire plain towards the dark hills. In 1282, Edward I instructed his local ally Roger Mortimer to widen the roads from Chester for strategic reasons.[1] This road is as wide as he could have wished. Room enough today for two lanes of Welsh livestock lorries, Polish artics and commuters shuttling between the cheaper housing of the hills and the better wages of the cities of the plain. As it crosses the Dee, a Red Dragon sign appears on the roadsign to your left, the Cross of St George dwindles in your rearview mirror, and the escarpment dividing Wrexham from the plain rises like a rampart. A couple of roundabouts, a slip road, '*Canol y Dref* / Town Centre', and you're in the centre of the capital of north Wales.

'Town' centre, rather than city centre. Despite its size – 42,000 people in the town, and 109,000 in the whole county borough – and its regional importance, Wrexham's not a city. It tried for city status in 2002 when a batch of such honours were up for grabs to mark the Queen's Golden Jubilee. But it lost out to Newport, which had three times the population. Wrexham is, however, far and away the biggest town in north Wales, and it has one feature that many cities conspicuously lack, namely a magnificent, towering church big enough to put some cathedrals in the shade.

But St Giles' Church isn't a cathedral. Even though it's one of the most impressive pieces of ecclesiastical architecture in Wales, and is named as one of the Seven Wonders of Wales in the late eighteenth century rhyme.

> Pistyll Rhaeadr and Wrexham steeple,
> Snowdon's mountain without its people,
> Overton yew trees, St Winefride's Well,
> Llangollen Bridge and Gresford bells.

No-one knows who wrote that, but it's worth a guess that he was from north Wales, as all the 'wonders' are in the north. It's also a fair bet he was from north east Wales, as six of the seven are there. And as four of the seven are in the Wrexham area, I think there's a strong case for him being a Wrexham man. Whoever he was, he was a savvy promoter. More than two centuries on, people are still dutifully travelling to visit the churches of Gresford and Overton even though there are more musical bells and much older yew trees to be had in Wales. The power of poetry. Or the power of doggerel, even.

The church itself was built in the late fifteenth century, and there was a move a century later to make it cathedral of St Asaph diocese. That came to nothing, but the church itself, with its giant perpendicular tower and its angel-studded wooden roof, is still the town's major landmark. From 1856, it had a rival when St Mark's Church was built at the other end of the town centre, with a two hundred foot spire, the highest in Wales, a full sixty-five feet higher than St Giles'. But that lasted barely a century; it was demolished in 1959 and replaced with a squat multi-storey car park ugly even by the standards of multi-storey car parks, but named, with brutal, unintended irony, 'St Mark's'.

The town centre doesn't have the same kind of architectural unity as somewhere like Chester, say. Nor was it a planned town, like Llandudno.[2] There was no all-powerful patron to demolish and rebuild in one dominant style. And there was no bonanza of industrial wealth to build a civic centre or monumental public buildings such as happened in Cardiff. Instead, Wrexham grew organically; a street here, a terrace there; factories, shops and homes squeezing into empty spaces in various styles: a bit of stolid Georgian, a few corners of fanciful Gothic, and large expanses of utilitarian Victorian Industrial, united only by the dominance of the local red brick, and a few highlights of black-and-white Cheshire-style half-timbered detail. Growing up, I was fortunate that my father, a quantity surveyor and the director of a building firm, had a strong interest in architecture, and would point out the features and periods represented in the townscape: the Georgian first-floor windows showing that the record shop was once a town house; the carved decorations above the newsagents, testifying to an earlier, grander purpose. The fascination of reading a community's history in the silent messages of its buildings has never left me.

The civic centre of Wrexham is the Guildhall at Llwyn Isaf, a long 1961 office block overlooking the former vicarage grounds. There's a Trumpton-style bandstand, a library, and a town hall balcony for waving at the crowds like a *generalissimo* on big occasions. Wrexham's *Casa Rosada*. Nearby are the law courts and the 1970s tower-block police station; the two linked by an underground tunnel to prevent inmates escaping in transit. Opposite is the Dorito-shaped parabolic roof of Wrexham Waterworld, the town's most controversial building when built as the council swimming baths in 1970.

But if Wrexham has a centre, it's not the official buildings, quiet park benches or trimmed municipal lawns. It's King Street, site of north

Wales' largest bus station, which decants and distributes people from all over the area – from leafy Acton and Garden Village to rocky Bwlchgwyn and Gwynfryn. As such it's the heart of the borough. Not beautiful, certainly, but alive. King Street is a planned terrace built in the early nineteenth century, but its original buildings have mostly now been replaced by cheaper twentieth century offices and shops. The bus station has been redeveloped from a rack of crack-kerbed, oil-stained lean-to shelters into a metallic-panelled central concourse with piped music and electronic destination boards, like an airport terminal without planes, and with the buses in slow, perpetual, rumbling orbit around it.

The one-way system here provides a loop for young scallies to circle the block in their customised Novas, bass volume thumping, eyes skimming the pavement at hemline level. Just behind King Street is a relic of earlier two-wheeled mating rituals; the old Majestic cinema, built in 1910 as a roller-skating rink and quickly converted into a cinema, local hormones finding better outlets in the warm intimate darkness than in the brightly-lit public circuit of the rink. It later became north Wales' largest picture house, an art deco palace seating 1770.[3] When it closed, the balcony was dismantled and reassembled as the stand at the town end of Wrexham FC's Racecourse ground. Those with longer memories called it the 'Majestic Stand', others called it the 'Pigeon Loft'. But it was no place for courting couples any more. As far as hormones go, it was testosterone-only. No handholding there. Bitten nails and clenched fists aplenty, though. The stand was eventually demolished. But the cinema building itself survived and now, renamed The Elihu Yale, after Wrexham's most famous son, founder of Yale University in America, it's

a Wetherspoons pub; a new generation of couples meeting over *lasagne al forno* and easy-drinking *pinot grigio*.

Crane's music shop used to stand in this street, a magnet alike for parents of precocious child pianists and for mooching teens dreaming of Fender Stratocasters. A connection with this shop once gave me a pang of *hiraeth* eight thousand miles away from Wales.

I was in Argentina in 2001

doing some work for the British
Council in the Welsh colony in
Patagonia, which had been
founded in the nineteenth century. I had left the lower Chubut
valley, the main Welsh settlement, and travelled by night bus
the five hundred miles west
across the desert to the offshoot
colony at Trevelin in the Andes.
There, I visited the local folk
museum: the usual collection of
agricultural implements and
handicrafts from pre-motor-car

days – not so far distant in that part of Argentina, where horseback is
still the easiest way to get around the hills. One of the prize exhibits was
an old-fashioned harmonium, of the sort once a status symbol in many
Welsh homes, the kind of asthmatic one-man orchestra you tried to coax
into wheezing a tune while giving it desperate CPR with the foot ped-
als. There was a plaque just above the keyboard. I looked a bit closer.
'Crane's, Wrexham,' it said. I couldn't help but wonder at the determination which had transported this windy wardrobe of an instrument
eight thousand miles by sea and then another five hundred by horse and
cart across a dangerous wilderness so that it could liven up the family
gatherings in some wood-built pioneer cabin. When they say they made
their own entertainment in those days, they meant it.

One of the pleasures of being in Patagonia is overhearing someone
speaking Welsh, and having to remind yourself you're actually in the
southern hemisphere, not in rural Denbighshire. You can hear Welsh
spoken in Wrexham too, of course. But at the moment, you're just as
likely to hear Polish. With an estimated ten thousand Poles in the borough, the language is not just audible but visible: shops and internet
cafes cater for the ex-pats; the library has a special Polish section;
bread shops advertise Polish favourites. For a town for whom
'Europe' used to mean the occasional foray into the Cup Winners'
Cup, the continent has suddenly come very close.

However, Regent Street has one, half-hidden memorial to someone
who tried to bring the continent closer in an earlier age. The arch in
Argyle Street has a plaque in memory of William Low,[4] the man who
tried to create the first channel tunnel. Low was a Scottish railway engineer who came to the Wrexham area with the coal industry, living first

at Llofft Wen, Coedpoeth, and later building a house near where Yale College stands today. In the mid nineteenth century, he formed the Channel Tunnel Company, which got French and British government backing and began work tunnelling from Kent. But the project was scuppered by the Franco-Prussian war, and had to be abandoned. Low did leave his legacy in Wrexham, though, by putting up Westminster Buildings, which spans Argyle Street, and which is a tunnel, of a kind.

POETRY AND PUBS

Just round the corner in Lord Street is Wrexham's most striking piece of public art, *The Arc*, by the Scottish sculptor David Annand.[5] It shows two life-size metal figures of a miner and a steelworker pulling the two halves of a steel arc towards unity. It's inscribed with a Welsh four-line *englyn* by the chaired bard Myrddin ap Dafydd, from Llanrwst.

> *Uwch y waedd, drwy'r gawod chwys – a helynt*
> *y morthwylion stormus,*
> *heibio'r awr sy'n bwyta brys*
> *mae tynfa yma at enfys.*

which means, roughly:

> Above the shout, the shower of sweat, and the clamour
> of thundering hammers,
> past the hour that devours haste,
> we reach to make a rainbow.

I once did a poetry reading at Wrexham Library Arts Centre with Myrddin and a couple of other poets. Afterwards, we went to look for a pub, and we walked past the sculpture, and Myrddin's poem. I knew it was there, but he didn't know that I knew. Modest, he didn't so much as stop to look at it.

We ended up that night in the Horse and Jockey in Regent Street. Wrexham's most distinctive pub, with its unique thatched roof. Restored after being gutted in a fire a few years ago, this pub, more than most, has reason to welcome the smoking ban.

Local folklore claims Wrexham has more pubs per head of population than anywhere else in Britain. It's not true, of course. There's no pub-to-population statistical unit somewhere producing useless figures of that kind, however gratifying they might be to local saloon-bar self-aggrandisement. And besides, I've heard the same claim made about every other town where I've ever stayed long enough to pick up the local booze-fuelled folklore: Cardiff, Merthyr Tydfil, Aberystwyth, Cambridge. They can't all have the highest ratio of public houses per head. But they all think they do.

Wrexham did, however, once have a subsidiary legend, which was more credible, and more provable: that Abbot Street had more pubs than any other street of similar length in the town. For a short street, it certainly had plenty. You could do a punishing pub crawl in fifty yards: The Bull, The Cannon, The Harp, The Goat, The Cymro Arms, The Hand, The Cross Foxes and the Old Swan.[6] Today it has just two, Sugar Reef, and the sole survivor from the old days: The Old Swan. Even in 1859, the Swan Brewery in Abbot Street, was called the *Old* Swan Brewery.

> The Old Swan Brewery, Wrexham. The Celebrity of the ALES of this Brewery has been acquired by the same means it is still maintained – attention being ESPECIALLY paid to make them suitable FOR FAMILY USE. No better testimonial can be given in favor of these ALES than that their purity, genuineness and general superiority have gained for them the patronage of most of the surrounding Clergy and Gentry. The Best TABLE BEER for ordinary use. In

quantities to suit the convenience of families, upon the most econom-
ical terms.
                                                    (Wrexham trade directory, 1859).

Its going to be ace, come down take a look for yourself
PHAT new system
cammo!!!
lazers!!
beer!
CRAZY PEOPLE!!!
★ I'll be there! as an alcoholic, gotta say it's always nice to see normal
people getting pissed-up and partying during daylight hours, and this
is as good a reason as any!
★ Would this be that small pub tucked away on Abbott st?
★ correct. it's down the little tunnel. CHEAP BOOZE!! + nuts and
crisps.
                        (dontstayin.com/uk/wrexham/the-old-swan/chat, 2007)

Maybe in the nineteenth century, Wrexham's reputation for high-
density boozing was deserved. By the middle of that century, as many
as one in twenty houses in Wrexham were licensed for the sale of
liquor.[7] Wrexham's historian A.H. Dodd commented: "This made the
regulation of drunkenness (combined as it was with an inbred
propensity to fisticuffs) a task beyond the powers of a scratch police
force."[8] Or as a commentator on the *Knowhere* webguide put it
recently: "For me there are just too many rednecks causing bother in
Wrexham town centre at night."[9]

George Borrow found the same when he visited in 1854, as
recorded in his classic travelogue, *Wild Wales*. He was warned against
walking out at night in parts of Wrexham, for fear drunken miners
would pick a fight with him. On his first morning in town, he went
out after breakfast and got talking to a group of local men:

I asked them if they were Welsh. 'Yes, sir,' said one, 'I suppose we are,
for they call us Welsh.' I asked if any of them could speak Welsh. 'No,
sir,' said the man, 'all the Welsh that any of us know, or indeed wish to
know, is "*Cwrw da*."' Here there was a general laugh. *Cwrw da* signi-
fies good ale…I was subsequently told that all the people of Wrexham
are fond of good ale.

Returning to Wrexham later, after a circular tour of north Wales, he encountered a young couple who confirmed his opinion:

> a young fellow of about eight-and-twenty, with a round face, fair
> flaxen hair, and rings in his ears; the female was a blooming buxom
> lass of about eighteen.
> 'I asked them if they were English.
> 'Aye, aye, master,' said the man; 'we are English.'
> 'Where do you come from?' said I.
> 'From Wrexham,' said the man.
> 'I thought Wrexham was in Wales,' said I.
> 'If it be,' said the man, 'the people are not Welsh; a man is not a
> horse because he happens to be born in a stable.'
> 'Is that young woman your wife?' said I.
> 'Yes;' said he, 'after a fashion'- and then he leered at the lass, and
> she leered at him.
> 'Do you attend any place of worship?' said I.
> 'A great many, master!'
> 'What place do you chiefly attend?' said I.
> 'The Chequers, master!'
> 'Do they preach the best sermons there?' said I.
> 'No, master! but they sell the best ale there.'
> 'Do you worship ale?' said I.
> 'Yes, master, I worships ale.'
> 'Anything else?" said I.
> 'Yes, master! I and my mort worships something besides good ale;
> don't we, Sue?' and then he leered at the mort, who leered at him, and
> both made odd motions backwards and forwards, causing the baskets
> which hung round them to creak and rustle, and uttering loud shouts
> of laughter, which roused the echoes of the neighbouring hills.

BREWERY SITES

During the Citizen's Band radio craze of the 1970s, every town had its
nickname. Real placenames were just too dull for the cowboy fantasy
world where lorry drivers, sales reps and radio hams exchanged crackly
messages in fake American accents. London was Noddy Town, for
instance, and Cardiff was Smoky Dragon (it still had a steelworks).
Industries were popular as airwaves alter egos: Bury St Edmunds was
Sugar Town, St Helen's was Glass Town; Northwich was Salt City. For
Wrexham, the CBers had only one choice – Lager Town.

Because Wrexham was Britain's lager capital. For nearly a century before lager became the drink of choice for a generation, Wrexham had specialised in a product most British drinkers only associated with foreign holidays.[10]

It all started in the nineteenth century when Ivan Levinstein and Otto Isler, two Manchester-based German immigrants, tried to replicate the lager-making conditions of their homeland in Wrexham, a town with a brewing industry dating back to the middle ages, and which, by the mid-nineteenth century, had nineteen breweries.[11] The newcomers felt the water quality of Pant y Golfen spring was as close as possible to that of Plzen in Bohemia, lager's spiritual home. They planned to store the beer in deep cellars in the Welsh hills, whose rock would be a natural refrigerator to maintain the minus-one-degree centigrade necessary for successful lager production.

But Bavaria has permanent Alpine snow to keep the *keller* cool. The would-be Bavaria in the Berwyns hadn't, and despite Levinstein and Isler building their own German-style *brauerei* in Central Street in 1881 – only the second lager brewery in Britain[12] – the company soon went into liquidation. The *Wrexham Advertiser* had already warned the enterprise of the warmer temperatures of Britain, and might have been forgiven a bit of *schadenfreude*. So much for your much-vaunted German efficiency.

But it wasn't over. Levinstein met Robert Graesser, a director of Monsanto, the Acrefair chemical company. Graesser determined to have a second crack at the lager challenge, this time using mechanical refrigeration technology. It worked.

But there was still a problem. Wrexham locals couldn't be weaned off their dark native ales onto this continental delicacy. Some of the attempts to persuade them to try the matured taste of lager sound as if the Germans had rather too sophisticated a view of the drinking habits of a Welsh mining and steel town: "You do not drink new wines! So why drink new beer?" or "It matures and becomes round in flavour. It is the champagne of beers." They even had to produce a leaflet entitled "What is Lager?" It looked like the idea was too far ahead of its time, and that the enterprise would fail again.

Then Graesser had a lucky break; travelling to America by sea, he found his beer kept its taste better on the voyage than those of his competitors. He decided to target the export market. With the British Empire at its height, and hundreds of thousands of ex-pats thirsty for a taste of home, Wrexham's lager business grew steadily. In 1898, a bottle was even found in the grounds of General Gordon's Palace in Khartoum, probably left there by the relief force sent thirteen years earlier to try, unsuccessfully, to rescue him from the army of the Mahdi.

The brewery expanded throughout most of the twentieth century, even surviving anti-German feeling during the two world wars. By the late 1940s, lager had long become a naturalised British drink, and the Wrexham company enjoyed its share of the growing market until eventually, bigger players – Ind Coope, Allied, Carlsberg Tetley – overtook it, bought it up, passed it between them like an unwanted grandparent and finally, in 2000, shut it down. The modern part of the brewery was demolished. In its place is a retail park: PC World; Au Naturale Interiors; SCS Great Sofas Great Prices. Only the original listed Bavarian-style building remains. Now available as modernised office space. Currently vacant.

If Wrexham Lager was the blond, confident continental, the town's other major brewery, Border, specialising in malty bitters and dark, sweet milds, was the swarthy, brooding native. Its advertising stressed its local roots rather than any exotic *mitteleurop* origins: 'The Prince of Ales,' 'Join the North Wales Borderers'. Border had its own pub on the premises: the Nag's Head.[13] The gloriously-named Johnny Basham, European Welterweight Boxing Champion, used to train here during the First World War, when stationed at Hightown Barracks. The Nag's Head was an institution, and the savvy drinker knew it served the cheapest pint in town; zero delivery costs keeping the price down. It was probably environmentally-friendly too, reducing the number of beer miles between brewery and boozer.

During the First World War, Border had gained an unexpected hit of free publicity when one of its motorised drays, requisitioned by the army, was damaged by a shell, and the photograph of this unlikely casualty was circulated widely. But patriotism couldn't protect it from the manoeuvring of brewing's rival Great Powers: Marstons, Burtonwood and Whitbread. In 1984, Marstons won, shelved its prior assurances of continued beer production at Wrexham, and closed the brewery six months later.

A campaign led by the then Wrexham MP, John Marek,

saved the brewery's giant decorated red brick chimney. The main brewery building itself survived too, converted, twenty years after its closure, into sixteen 'high quality apartments'; three 'exclusive penthouses' and, two 'private roof gardens'. For generations, brewing had given the atmosphere of the whole town the fragrance of hops. It was unpleasant to some, pleasing to most, and it's now, for all, no more than an evocative memory. Any surviving CBers – there are some – would be hard-pressed to find a one-word summary for Wrexham now. "Breaker, breaker, just coming up to Luxury Apartment Town." No, not quite the same ring.

EAGLES MEADOW

Apartments are Wrexham's new cash crop. Where the borough's residents once dug down for its mineral wealth, now they build up for the lucrative air rights. There's gold in them there empty spaces. And until it became the centre of a huge shopping and apartment development, there was no space in Wrexham town centre quite as empty as Eagles Meadow. This oval of land behind the Wynnstay Arms Hotel, formerly the Eagles Hotel, was always a public space for horse fair, bowling green, open market or travelling funfair.

In the days before malls, fairs were highly-lucrative commercial franchises, strictly controlled by the authorities. Wrexham had one as early as 1391, and by 1489, the rights were held by the Crown. Every Monday, until only a few years ago, Eagles Meadow would become a tented village of market stalls and vans. Luxury was a spongy Westlers hamburger from a caravan, or a bag of chips from the on-site chippy. Now the site's a giant retail, leisure and residential complex, with forty-odd shops, a thousand parking spaces, tenpin bowling, bars, restaurants and an eight-screen multiplex. All built round a Spanish Steps theme and a water feature.

Mall replaces mart. It's tempting to sneer at one and elegise the other. Tempting, but too easy. Swapping a weekly market for a towering multi-purpose shopping centre is a change only in degree not in character. They'll even be bowling there still.

Besides, the process has been going on for years. As the fairs waned, their prime sites went to more permanent and profitable enterprises, most notably the town's three magnificent Victorian covered markets: the Meat Market, Butter Market and Vegetable Market. The largest, the airy, high-roofed Vegetable Market, was demolished in the 1980s and eventually replaced by a shopping precinct. The traders were displaced, like victims of a Soviet removal programme, to the other side of Chester Street, to a replacement building, called, with ominous Stalinist overtones, The People's Market, a utilitarian, low-ceilinged space, seemingly weighed down by the tiers of the multi-storey car park above it. The redbrick and cast-iron Meat Market and Butter Market still survive. Two out of three. Meat, Butter. But no Veg.

One feature of the days of Wrexham's travelling fairs survives too: the Simons Funfair, a fifth-generation family business begun as a travelling menagerie and 'living pictures' bioscope by John Litchfield Simons. He died in his caravan on Wrexham's Beast Market in 1903, leaving his widow and twelve children to continue taking the business round the festivals and fair-days of north Wales towns.[14] Pushed from its traditional location on Eagles Meadow, the Simon's fair continues, albeit relocated. It returns to Wrexham each holiday; a bit of a vagabond, but always home for Christmas and Easter.

Next door to Eagles Meadow was the Beast Market, where farmers would come from the hills every Monday, tweed-jacketed, flat-capped, discussing the prices of ewes and lambs in Welsh over the metal-railed animal pens.[15] This too had been a public space since medieval times, reserved for fairs, markets and – in the days when an afternoon's entertainment could consist of watching someone being killed – executions. The most famous of these was four centuries ago, when Richard Gwynn suffered

what the Catholic Church classed as a martyr's death.

Gwynn was only in his late twenties when he died here. He'd converted to Roman Catholicism at a time when, in the wake of the Protestant Reformation, that was regarded as treason and virtually guaranteed a death sentence. That sentence was carried out on Gwynn at the Beast Market, on 17 October 1584, and as slowly as the executioners could manage. If you've seen the end of *Braveheart*, you'll get the idea. He was the first, but not the last, Welsh Catholic martyr. The Pope made him a saint in 1970, and he's commemorated in the town's Roman Catholic Cathedral, which preserves an armbone said to have been rescued from when his dismembered quarters were displayed around north Wales as a warning.[16] The site of the execution is probably under the present-day Tesco supermarket. But there's no memorial, just a metal bay for empty trolleys, and till receipts blowing under the car tyres.

HIGHTOWN

There was a fight outside 'Jacko's Chippy.' It was late on a Saturday afternoon, and I'd made my way up to Brynycabanau Road in Hightown to visit the former site of my old comprehensive school, Ysgol Morgan Llwyd.

They were two youths. Anything between fifteen and nineteen. The heavy-set one already had a bloody nose. The thinner one was taunting him, egged on by a circle of gobby girls. A fringe of smaller kids circled outside, bikes temporarily abandoned, eyes shining. Behind them, the school-age population of Hightown Flats was pouring out to watch. I stopped the car. To intervene or not?

It looked like the dispute was over a bicycle. It lay at the centre of the circle as the two fighters manoeuvred round it like girls round dancefloor handbags. Was that worth risking injury for? And they weren't doing one another any real damage. I decided I'd only do anything if one of them went down and the other started doing him some serious harm. In the meantime, from the safety of my car. I called the police.

'How many are there?' said the young woman's voice.

'Two fighting. About thirty watching. More coming.'

'Ages?'

'Older teens. Seventeen maybe.'

'Can you see any weapons?'

Sensible question. She'd obviously done this before.

'No. No weapons.'

'OK. Stay where you are. We'll send a car.'

By this time, a woman, not worried about becoming the subject of an attack herself, had confronted the group, yelling at them to stop. And a couple of minutes later, the police sirens sent the crowd vanishing back into Hightown Flats as though a film had been reversed. The loser picked up the disputed bike and trailed away.

The scene would confirm many people's stereotypes about Hightown Flats. They were built in the 1960s on a triangle of land on the site of Gatefield, the home of Thomas Edgworth, Wrexham's first mayor. As blocks of flats go, they're not the worst: an assemblage of light-grey deck-access rectangles connected by walkways. They're only five storeys high, and are Wrexham's only experiment with high-density housing. Something to be grateful for? Not for Borras Hwfa, aka 'Gog Almighty', one of the regulars on Skyscrapercity.com, a website devoted to the joys of tower blocks:

> As for Wrexham – not a single tower block I'm afraid – maybe that's why I grew up with the fascination. If there is one place in North Wales which would have them, you think it would be here wouldn't you? But alas, no.

Alas? But he ventures into Hightown Flats early one morning ("about 8.00am – ...whilst the skagheads were still lying around in their dog's poo") to photograph them for the benefit of his fellow enthusiasts. They love it. As property porn goes, this is very much the 'fetish' end of the market.

Brynycabanau Road gets its name ('Hill of the Cabins'), so legend has it, from the time when wooden buildings were erected here to isolate plague victims. When I attended Ysgol Morgan Llwyd here in the 1970s, that legend had become confused in my mind with the real wooden cabins in which the school was partially based. In the time-honoured tradition of catering for Welsh-medium education, the school had been allocated buildings surplus to requirements: in this case, the former Hermitage ex-World-War-Two military camp.[17] By my time, a purpose-built school block had been put up, but the gymnasium and many other buildings were still wooden-walled army-surplus, an irony in a school whose nationalist ethos regarded the British Armed Forces as just one more oppressive arm of a British state which had forced Welsh speakers into a position where they were expected to be grateful for leftovers. When I told the careers officer I planned to join the Army – to be a rebel in Morgan Llwyd you had to be inventive – I was told the school would give me no help to join the forces of the English Crown.

No such scruples have affected the scores of thousands of Wrexham people who have joined the armed forces over the centuries. Just opposite the former Hermitage camp is Hightown Barracks, the old headquarters of the Royal Welch Fusiliers, formed in 1689, and serving in every major conflict involving British forces since then. The legions of Royal Welchmen who fought in World War One passed through Hightown Barracks on their way to the conflict, where ten thousand of them died. Their World War Two counterparts did the same, another thirteen hundred of them dying. Currently, the building houses some Territorial Army Units. Soft-skinned lorries and other military hardware are positioned inside the barbed-wire compound. But today, it looked like the only fighting seen around here was outside the chippy.

CAIA PARK

There was some fighting in nearby Caia Park in June 2003, though. And of a kind which made headlines across Britain. It wasn't the scale of the riots that made them notorious – at their height, two hundred people fought with about twenty-five police. It wasn't their severity either – this wasn't Toxteth, Brixton or Broadwater Farm. The headlines were because this particular cocktail of hot heads and hot summer nights contained the crucial element that is the journalistic equivalent of a heroin hit – race.

It began as a clash between local youths and a group of Iraqi Kurdish men, refugees who were the subject of rumours and resentment. When locals attacked and badly injured a Kurdish man, Hoshank Baker Kader, a group of his friends armed themselves with knives and improvised bludgeons and attacked the Red Dragon pub, where they thought the assailants were hiding. The locals fought back with snooker cues and chair legs. When police arrived, they themselves became the focus of the locals' anger. The violence continued sporadically for two days.

For weeks afterwards, Caia Park was the centre of the nation's collective anxiety over racial issues. The BNP tried to capitalise; locals tried to downplay; distant commentators wrung their hands. But the incident proved ultimately unsatisfying to those looking for clear-cut victims and villains, and the media spotlight moved on, seeking simpler stories. The Kurds moved on too. The court cases dragged on for months, with fifty-one people – locals and Kurds – eventually getting a collective total of eighty years' custody.

It had all looked much brighter when Queen's Park – the estate's former name – was laid out just after World War Two, drawing on the best of Wrexham's successful experience of creating garden villages to replace industrial slums. W. Alister Williams' *A Wrexham Encyclopaedia* notes the optimism and satisfaction the project created: there would be shops, schools, sports facilities and churches; streets would follow land contours so that people could have a view; all houses would have gardens. Reviewing the project in 1960, Alderman Herbert Jennings felt well pleased: "I believe we shall progress towards completion of as good an estate and as happy a community as can be found anywhere."[18]

Years later, Queen's Park had attracted the kind of reputation that outsiders' snobbery delights in attributing to council estates, and which insiders' inverted snobbery delights in exaggerating. When it was renamed Caia Park, it was meant to be a new start, shaking off the bad reputation of the past. After all, the area had some distinguished connections. The former American President, Richard Nixon, could trace his descent from John Puleston, a fifteenth century member of a family who lived at Hafod y Wern, just behind where the Red Dragon pub now stands.[19] Now that this location has been a site of events which seem likely to connect the words 'Caia Park' with 'riot' permanently, maybe it's time to consider renaming the estate again. Something that wouldn't suggest criminality and dark hidden secrets. The Richard Nixon Housing Estate perhaps? Then again, perhaps not.

YO! WREXHAM!

"Nice to see another Scouser here."

The smiling lady had stopped me at the door as I left an event where I had just given a reading. She was all set to swap reminiscences about Merseyside. I had to disappoint her.

"I'm sorry. I'm not a Scouser."

"But...your accent...?"

"I know."

I know all right. When I was growing up in Wrexham in the 1970s, the Merseyside accent had already spread into north east Wales, squeezing the vowels of the natives into what seem to be diluted but still recognisable Merseyside sounds, softening the 't's to 'tch's, and grinding the 'ck's into gutteral 'ch's. By today, Mersey Estuary English has flowed right along the north Wales coast at least as far as Bangor, but in those less mobile days it was confined to the border areas. That meant that Wrexhamites' accents involved their owners in many wearisome explanations of their origins both to sceptical fellow Welsh people and would-be seekers of Scouse solidarity.

But however similar to Liverpudlian the Wrexham accent may sound to the untutored ear, it's unmistakeable to those familiar with the area. I found this out early. Aged eighteen, and looking to unwind after my A-levels, I'd gone on a walking holiday by myself in the west highlands of Scotland. I booked into a guest house in Oban. At breakfast, the waitress came over and asked me what I'd like to eat.

"I'll have the full Scottish breakfast and a pot of tea please."

After she'd gone back to the kitchen, a middle-aged man on a table at the other end of the room looked up.

"What part of Wrexham are you from?"

He was a Scouser, evacuated to Wrexham during the war. My few words to the waitress had been enough to place me.

Not that my accent was as broad as some. As a child of a middle-class home, I never acquired the habit of calling people 'la' – short for 'lad' – or pronouncing 'you' as 'yo'. But the accent, although muted, was there. It spreads across most social boundaries in the area, even those dividing English speakers and Welsh speakers. Unlike some areas of Wales, where the communal strength of Welsh presses that language's distinctive sounds into people's English pronunciation, in Wrexham the pressure is the other way round, and it's almost impossible to tell who's Welsh-speaking by listening to their English accents.

It's a frequent surprise to find that someone who sounds as if they'd be quite at home on *Brookside* is actually also quite comfortable in the language of *Pobol y Cwm*.

Wrexham has fewer hang-ups about Welsh than might be expected. Historically, Denbighshire council, like neighbouring Flintshire, was an early pioneer of bilingual education – the first Welsh-medium secondary school in Wales was set up at Glan Clwyd in Rhyl in 1956, and Wrexham now has several Welsh-medium primaries as well as Ysgol Morgan Llwyd secondary. This attitude contributed to a generally tolerant atmosphere. The scoreboard at the Racecourse football ground carries bilingual messages. Nurses in the town's Maelor General Hospital routinely check patients' language preferences when they're admitted, and staff who can speak Welsh wear a badge to show they can do so. You might be ill, but at least you can be ill in Welsh. These things matter.

But that shouldn't be taken to mean that Welsh is more than an undertone here – unremarked, and unresented, perhaps, but an undertone all the same. English is the unquestioned *lingua franca*. How to view that? Pessimistically or optimistically?

For the poet Bryan Martin Davies, who spent thirty years as a teacher in Wrexham, the glass of Border beer was half-empty. For him, the language was like snow clinging stubbornly to the hills at Gwynfryn and Bwlchgwyn in the west, but only visiting the town in the odd market-day flurry, to melt away quickly again, unlamented.[20] For Aled Lewis Evans, long-time Wrexham resident and tireless chronicler of the weirdnesses of border life in his poems and stories in both languages, the glass is half-full. As a teacher of Welsh, and promoter of the culture in all its forms, he has to be optimistic. For instance, he's noted how many people who claim not to speak a word of the language, nonetheless pepper their speech with words and phrases direct from Welsh.

Where other people might say 'in'it?' as the all-purpose gap-filling interrogative, many Wrexham people say 'nye', derived from the Welsh '*yn ai*?' Other similar words are in frequent use by people who are not themselves Welsh-speaking: '*bonc*' for a hillock or mound; 'cacky monkey' for a briar burr, derived from the Welsh '*cacamwci*'; and '*cyth*' meaning devilment, derived from the Welsh '*cythraul.*' In some cases, even some of the mutation system has leaked into English, meaning that 'the tram' becomes 'the dram', and – staying with modes of transport – the town's once-ubiquitous Crosville buses, when prefaced with the definite article, became, for many people, 'the *G*rosville'.

Linguists would call these 'relic terms', of course, words from a dead culture living out an afterlife for a generation or two in the speech which has superseded them. Ultimately destined to vanish.

Except Welsh doesn't vanish. The figures for the number of Welsh speakers in the area remain stubbornly steady, even registering a slight growth. The 2001 census showed 21,822 people out of the 124,024 residents of the county borough able to speak, read or write Welsh, with a further couple of thousand able to understand the spoken language.[21] That represents about eighteen per cent of the population; not high compared to places like Gwynedd, but nothing less than amazing considering the proximity of the English border. There are wards of Wrexham, like rural Glyn Ceiriog and industrial Ponciau, where more than a third of people are Welsh-speaking. And the town itself – its shops, football club and hospital particularly – draws people from the Welsh-speaking hinterland as far west as Bala.

Not vanishing then. But neither is the language here likely to see the dramatic resurgence witnessed in Cardiff, where migrants from the north and west of Wales have swelled the capital's Welsh-speaking population, and where the language has in recent years become much more visible and audible. Wrexham's not quite ready for that.

A few years ago, the council experimented with an electronic talking rubbish bin set up outside the King Street bus station. When any litter was deposited in its mouth, it responded, in a metallic voice with a strong north Wales accent: "On behalf of the council, thank you for keeping our borough tidy."

Of course, being an official announcement by a public body, this message, in accordance with the 1993 Welsh Language Act, had to be done bilingually. So it was accompanied by the same message in Welsh. Aled Lewis Evans recorded the reaction of two of the bin's startled users:

"You what? He's proper Welsh, ain't he?"

"Who?"

"The bleedin' bin."[22]

MOLD ROAD, RACECOURSE GROUND

If people outside Wales have heard of Wrexham, it's usually for one reason alone: football. Sport has traditionally given working-class kids a way to fame, and football gave this industrial town its collective ticket out of obscurity. For most of its history, Wrexham AFC was one of only four Welsh clubs in the English Football League, and despite its near-permanent position in the old Third Division, the club punched well above its weight in cup competitions, bringing down First Division titans like Newcastle, and even, on one unforgettable occasion in 1992, Arsenal. And thanks to its success in the Welsh Cup, Wrexham also qualified regularly for the European Cup Winners' Cup, giving the town a heady taste of Continental competition every few years. The adage that football is more than a game was never more true than in Wrexham.

Wrexham FC is one of Wales' oldest clubs, formed in 1872 (a year before the date on the club's badge) when cricketers playing at the town's multi-purpose racecourse site on Mold Road wanted something to do during the winter. The club came into being at the Turf Hotel, which doubled for many years as a changing room and mini-grandstand: it had its own balcony at the back of the pub, from which a select group of regulars could buy tickets to watch the game, pint-in-hand, a privilege no other league club could offer, and one which only ended in the 1990s, when the new Pryce Griffiths Stand blocked the view.

The Racecourse, for many years, until it was superseded by Cardiff's Millennium Stadium, was a major venue for Welsh soccer internationals, and saw some famous victories. The most memorable, for me, was in November 1975, in a European qualifier, when Wales beat Austria one-nil thanks to a goal from local boy Arfon Griffiths, then enjoying an indian summer as an international. There were nearly 28,000 people packed into the ground, and when the goal went in, the roar could be heard four miles away.

I count myself lucky my adolescence coincided with the greatest days in Wrexham FC's history: the legendary 1977-78 season, when the club won promotion to the old Second Division for the first time. I used to watch the games with my father, brother and uncle from the old wooden-seated Plas Coch stand, and later, from the paddock below. We'd follow them to away games, red and white scarves clamped

in the Cortina windows. The previous season, the club had suffered a heartbreaking disappointment, missing out on promotion at the last minute when success had seemed certain. Grown men cried. They cried again in 1977-78, but this time for a different reason, as Wrexham crowned a glorious season by securing promotion with a thumping 7-1 victory over Rotherham. They went on to win the league championship, and on the way had a spectacular cup run in which they defeated First Division opponents. I was fourteen, obsessed with the club, counting the days to the next game, and hoarding cuttings and photographs as though my life depended on it. When we were promoted, I thought life couldn't get any better. I think I was right.

Certainly, things never got any better for Wrexham. They quickly slumped back to the Third Division, then the Fourth, and despite occasional highlights like the Arsenal win in 1992, it seemed they'd returned to their level as lower-division strugglers with the odd flash of brilliance.

But that state seemed like a happy dream compared with the nightmare which started in 2002 when the ground was sold to property developer Alex Hamilton, who wanted to move the club from the site it had occupied for a hundred and thirty years. A legal battle followed, and the club went into administration. If that wasn't bad enough, the Football League had just introduced a new rule in which clubs which went into administration were docked ten points. Wrexham were the first victims of the punishment, which ensured their relegation to League Two, the old Fourth Division. The club and its fans eventually won a protracted law suit with Mr Hamilton, got

control of the ground, got new owners and got out of administration. But the damage had been done, and the off-field troubles had translated into a disastrous league position in 2007 in which they faced the serious prospect of relegation from the Football League and into the outer darkness of the Conference.

That was the situation when I went to the Racecourse in February to watch the Dragons play Wycombe Wanderers in company with one of the club's most loyal supporters, Terry Heath, one of the leaders of the fans' fund-raising efforts to help the club out of its trouble. He's watched Wrexham from the Kop, the all-standing terraced Crispin Lane end of the ground, since he was five. Forty-one years. And he's not the only one to show that kind of commitment. I meet him in the club shop where he helps out selling memorabilia: mugs, scarves, air-fresheners, all with the club badge. I consider buying the air-freshener, but then I remember that my car spends most of its life parked in Cardiff streets. I'd get plenty of fresh air with a broken windscreen. The shop's selling CDs of the song which was composed during Wrexham's promotion season, 'Wrexham is the Name.' Sung to the tune of 'Men of Harlech', it's etched in the memory of everyone who lived through that period: "Here they come, the might-y champ-ions / Raise your voic-es to the an-them, / March-ing like a might-y ar-my / Wrex-ham is the name." Better than the original 'Men of Harlech' in my opinion. Nearly thirty years on, it's still selling.

It's years since I've been on the Kop. We crank through the same turnstiles I used as a boy. I stood here for that Austria game in 1975, arriving ages before the kick-off in order to grab a place on one of the coveted concrete pillars along one side of the terrace, in order to see over the heads of the crowd. The concrete pillars are still there, but there's no need to stand on them today. There's a bare three thousand people here. A man passes me in a dark suit and red tie. He's wearing a white carnation and carrying a pint. On his way to or from a match of a different kind. His own maybe. Clearly, for the time being, the game is taking priority.

But it's not going well for Wrexham. The defence is leaky, and by early in the second half, Wycombe are leading 2-0. Then there's a commotion on the pitch near the Pryce Griffiths stand. A Wycombe player goes down. Wrexham fans think he's shamming, and barrack him. The physio attends the fallen player as his teammates mob the referee, demanding a sending-off. The injured player has to leave the pitch before play can resume. It's the law. As he gets to the edge of the pitch, some Wrexham fans take the opportunity to barrack him some more. They leave their seats and crowd up to the fence, shouting, pointing, gesturing from behind a wall of yellow-jacketed stewards. They're trying to goad a response which will damage Wycombe's chances. They get one, not from the player, but from the Wycombe keeper, who loses his cool and blasts the ball at the barrackers. He's a keeper, used to kicking for distance, and the ball misses, hitting a group of seated fans high up in the stand, who were not barracking. The keeper's sent off. The fans return to their seats, job done.

With their opponents down to ten men, Wrexham hopes rise. But even with a replacement keeper they still need to get their shots on target. They don't; the scoreline stays the same, and the Dragons slip a little closer to the danger zone.

A friend of Terry's stops to talk to him. He's an RAF man, just back from Iraq. Stationed in Basra and enjoying it. He's off for his second tour of duty soon, and is looking forward to going. After a two-nil defeat on a freezing February afternoon, I don't blame him. Terry goes back to the shop. There's merchandise to sell, every penny helps. If loyalty were hard cash, then Wrexham would be in the Premiership.

Red bricks[23]

compiled from inscriptions on
commemorative bricks at the Racecourse Ground

Supporters.
Wrexham Supporter
Loyal Supporters,
Loyal Supporter, (x 3)

Wrexham Fan 1999
Wrexham No 1 Fan 6.7.99
Dedicated since '91
Fan since 1977
Supporter 1975-
Red since 20.4.74
Loyal Red 1968
Fan since 1968
Cefnogwr ers 1968
Number 1 Fan 1967
Fan for life 17.2.66
Loyal Red 1966-99
Loyal since 1963
Follower 4.6.61
Forever Wrexham 1958
Loyal Fan, 1957

Saw his first match 10.9.55
Fan since 1950,
Forty Glorious Years!
Supporter 50 years 1950-2000
Fan from 1948
Wrexham Fan 1937
Supporter 1936-1980
Supporter 1936-85
Supporter 1927-87
Made in Wales 1917-97
Wrexham Fan 1912-98

No 1 Fan, (x2)
No 1 Fans
No 1 Fan 1940-1996,
No 1 Female Fan
No 1 Fan in Ruthin
No 1 Dad Steward and Fan

Wxm Fans,
Loyal Fan
Loyal Wrexham Fan
True Wrexham Fan
A true Wrexham Fan
Wxm Fan Forever
A fan for always
True 40 yr fan
Fifty Years a fan
50 years following the Reds
Lifetime supporter
Lifetime supporters
Lifelong followers
Lifelong supporter (x3)
Lifelong fan (x7)
Wrexham til I die (x6)
Wrexham till we die (x2)
5.11.57 Till Death
Fan from Afar
In exile S. Wales.
Still a fan
Supporters from above

Reds
True Red
True Reds
A Red Forever
Red Forever (x 3)
Forever Red, (x2)
Forever Reds,
Reds Forever, (x 5)
Long Live the Reds
Always Red (x2)
A true Red always
Up the Reds (x2)
Up the Reds Forever,
Red is in our Blood
Proud to be in Red
Red Through and Through
Born a Red 1973
3 generations of Reds
True Red and Gent
Long Live the Reds
C'mon you Reds (x 3)
Come on you Reds, (x 7)
Red Army
Red Army 2000
Red Army Forever
Gitit Red Army
Reds Rule
Super Reds, (x 2),
Simply Reds
Reds for Life,
Red til I'm Dead, (x 2)

I was there
Cymru 1999
Sing it proud 99,
Season 1998-99
19 Luvly Jubbly 98
Wrexham 2 – 1 Arsenal
1977-78 The Best
Joey, Mickey, Dixie, Thank You
For all the good times

The Good and Bad Times
Let the Good Times Roll

Wrecsam am byth (x 11)
Cymru am Byth (x5)
Cymru am Byth WFC
Coch am byth (x2)
Cefnogwyr am Byth,
Byddin goch am byth

Supporting Wrexham
Proud to support
I Love Wrexham
Wxm FC Pride of Wales
The best team
Wales No 1 Team
Tim Gorau Cymru
WFC Forever,
Wrexham Forever (x 11)
Wxm Forever
Forever Wrexham, (x 3)
Wrexham Now and Always
Made in Wrexham,
Wrexham at Heart
Born & Bred Wxm Fan
Wrexham Barmy Mad

Born Welsh
Proud to be Welsh (x 3)
Welsh Dragon
Cymro i'r Carn
Rhyfelwyr Cymreig
Diolch i'r Cochion
O bydded i'r heniaith barhau
Dwi'n casau Caer

Still on the Kop,
Forever on the Kop
Always Watching
Forever Trying
Still Waiting

I can no longer claim to be the world's biggest soccer fan. I've lived in south Wales for twenty years, and getting to Wrexham games hasn't been easy. But I've never been tempted to shift my allegiance elsewhere. I can never understand how people who come from one town can support teams from somewhere else. Like the legions of people from north Wales who support English Premier League teams – Liverpool, Everton, Manchester United – even holding season tickets and travelling for hours just to get to the home games. In the process they drive past Wrexham, which needs their support a sight more than Man U does. I agree with Frank Skinner: the only way to decide your soccer loyalty is with a map of your home town and a ruler to find the nearest football club to your house. If more people did that, then Wrexham's fortunes would be a whole lot brighter. Maybe sports lessons in north Wales schools should include some simple geography as well, using maps and rulers.

My attendance at Wrexham games lapsed once I moved south. However, no such backsliding has affected *Cochion Caerdydd*, the Cardiff Reds, a sleeper cell of Wrexham fans operating in deep cover within enemy territory. They may not be in north Wales any more, but they don't let that stop them following Wrexham. They were formed through people getting together on Wrexham's *Red Passion* fans' website, and they arrange trips to Wrexham's away games within reach of Cardiff: London, the Borders, the West Country, and, on the night I joined, them, Newport, where Wrexham were playing in the Welsh Premier Cup.

I used the internet to make the arrangements to meet the Cardiff Reds' founder and organiser, Rhys Wynne. As we discussed meeting in the Newport FC social club for a drink before the game, the question arose of how we would recognise one another. Helpfully, he sent me a picture of himself on Flikr.com, the photo-sharing website. Balding bloke. Thirties. Clean shaven. Fine. I consider sending a photograph of myself in response, but then I realise there's no need to bother. He's a football fan, so I only need to say one thing. I look like Gary Lineker.

There's no point in trying to hide the fact. Ever since my hair started turning grey I've borne a strong resemblance to the former England striker turned ubiquitous football pundit and cult-figure Walkers Crisps frontman. "Hey Gary! Got any crisps!" people shout when I walk into a pub. When I go out in town, people nudge one another and point; turn round to look at me, then turn round again for another look. Usually, the younger they are, and the more alcohol they've consumed, the likelier they are to shout something. But age is no barrier. I once delivered a lecture in Aberystwyth to a group of volunteers for community newspapers. The average age of the people must have been sixty-plus. Afterwards, two ladies, well into their seventies, approached me. Congratulations on the speech, I assumed. Some supplementary questions, maybe. No. Holding one another's arms and giggling like schoolgirls, they asked me, in Welsh: "Has anyone ever told you that you look like Gary Lineker?"

They've told me all right. All the time. And they all reckon they're the first ones to think of it. It's got so bad that if I see a group of males between the ages of eight and twenty-five – the ones most likely to heckle – I'll cross the road to avoid them and the comments they're bound to make. I've even developed my own line of weary witticisms for when I'm paying a bill and waitresses tell me who I look like. "Sorry," I tell them: "If I was Gary Lineker you'd be getting a bigger tip." It doesn't help that the man's image is *everywhere*. Match of the Day, the World Cup, TV adverts, posters on buses, on bus shelters, on hoardings. Comic Relief trailers. Even stand-up cardboard cutouts in supermarkets. I get all the hassle of fame with none of the income.

Some people also clearly think that I *am* Gary Lineker. They look. Look again. Call their friends over surreptitiously. Then they *all* look. And have a whispered consultation. "Yes it is" "No it isn't." And look again.

Which is what the lady clearing tables did when I walked into Newport FC's social club to meet the Cardiff Reds. She stopped what she was doing, shocked; her face looked as if she'd seen a ghost. But even a ghost would have been more likely to appear there than Gary Lineker. He's probably at home counting his millions, not slogging down the M4 to watch a non-league side slug it out with a relegation-threatened club for the prize of the Welsh Premier Cup. After a while, she stops staring and goes back to her work, although she does turn and give me another good look, just to make sure.

I catch up with Rhys Wynne and his small group. Rhys is from Prion near Denbigh, and tells me he was brought up supporting Everton, something which was common in his home village. Neighbouring villages supported Liverpool, entire communities adopting an allegiance to a distant metropolis. But he experienced a conversion to supporting Wrexham and still does so even though he's lived in Cardiff since 1999. He works as a private-sector officer for *Menter Iaith Caerffili*, promoting the Welsh language in the Rhymney Valley like a latter-day missionary.

That's a job that needs faith. So is the task of supporting Wrexham on a night like this. Newport County, once a Football League club like Wrexham, and representing a much bigger town – or a city as it became a few years ago – are now exiled in the Conference, playing the likes of Kidderminster, Crawley and Stevenage in front of crowds whose numbers you can count, and in an atmosphere where the players make more noise than the fans. It seems like a grim warning of the fate that could await Wrexham.

A villainous wind drives across the unsheltered terraces, whipping little knots of plastic cups and chip trays into mini trash-tornadoes in the concrete corners of the Newport Stadium. It blows players' throw-ins straight back into touch, boomerangs high passes back on themselves cartoonishly, turns goal kicks into space shots.

There are about seven of the Cardiff Reds here tonight, including Rhys: one from Caernarfon, one from Denbigh, one from Ruthin, one from Mold, two brothers from Port Talbot. None actually from Wrexham itself. In some cases, the allegiance seems to be genetic. Although Port Talbot is the home town of the two brothers, their father's from Wrexham. In another case, a fan comes because his grandfather is from Wrexham. They carry the loyalty in them like an inherited trait. My daughter, who's come with me tonight, has it too. Her classmates support the Cardiff Bluebirds. She tells them, apologetically, that she supports Wrexham, "because of Dad".

Rhys has promised to text a friend with the scores. He can text the first two in a single message because Wrexham's opener and Newport's leveller, a penalty, come within a minute of one another. The Newport fans have come to life now.

I was already feeling exposed, having reached the terraces through a scattering of predictable comments: "Hey it's Gary Lineker! Hur, hur!" "Hey Gary! Hur, hur, hur!"

Now, among this small knot of Wrexham supporters, I feel more self-conscious still. The freezing terraces are echoing with feral, tribal, choral obscenities. A chip thrown from behind me hits me on the shoulder. I ignore it. Most of the chants are simple – very simple – communal or personal abuse. But one Newport fan standing by himself near to me seems to have developed a more positive line of exhortation.

"Talk to one another'" he said, with quiet assurance, as though the players forty yards away could hear him.

"Give. Give."

He continued, a counselling counterpoint to the neanderthal hostility pulsing around him.

"Let it go."

"It's yours. Take it."

Newport take the lead. Wrexham heads go down. My daughter's getting bored. But on the way here, I'd stopped at a garage and stocked up for this very eventuality. I reach into my pocket and give her a packet of sweets, and then fetch out a bag of crisps for myself. As I do so, my heart sinks. I should have thought. They're Walkers. I try to hide the label as I eat them.

The final whistle. Wrexham are out of the cup. The giantkillers killed. The home fans go wild. The tannoy announcer gives the official attendance: 774. It's 776 actually, I think, recalling that no-one had actually taken any money from my daughter and I as we made our way into the ground. At least I didn't pay to see Wrexham lose. It's small consolation. The Newport fans stay to celebrate. The Wrexham fans take their way home silently. Underfoot, the terraces are littered with squashed chips. And Walkers bloody crisps.

BROOK STREET, TOWN HILL

It was always a case of mixed feelings that the Football Association of Wales had its headquarters in Wrexham. Great that Wrexham's status as an international venue was underlined; not so great that the address was 'Fairy Road'. Not only was it a tempting joke for more homophobic football fans – yes, there were some – but it also suggested something too light and insubstantial. Rather like Welsh hopes of qualifying for a major competition. The connection came to an end when, like so many national institutions, the FA eventually joined the drift to Cardiff, moving to its new headquarters in the neutrally-named Westgate Street in the capital in the 1980s.[24]

The 'Fairy' actually refers to the supposed otherworld origin of a Bronze Age burial mound which is still preserved here, and which local legend claimed was a favourite site of dancing for *Y Tylwyth Teg*, the

Fair Folk. In 1882, a local builder and mayor of Wrexham, W.E. Samuel, bought the area to develop it for housing. He supervised an excavation of the mound, finding human remains and a pottery urn. He preserved the mound itself, and its associated 'fairy' oak tree, and named the house 'Fairy Mount'.

Opposite, the elegant Belmont Hotel also takes its name from the 'fairy mount.' Homely, friendly, it's the venue for meetings of 'Cymdeithas Owain Cyfeiliog', the local literary society for Welsh speakers. Appropriate that a pub should host a society named after a poet whose only surviving work is a drinking-song.

Owain ap Gruffudd ap Maredudd (c.1130-1197), known as Owain Cyfeiliog, was one of the most powerful Welsh princes of his day, and was a poet and patron of poets. The only one of his pieces to survive, 'Hirlas Owain',[25] 'Owain's drinking-horn', is regarded as a classic. It records a successful raid in 1155 in which Owain rescued his brother from prison in Maelor, or 'Maelawr' as the spelling of the time has it. He toasts his war-band, greeting each in turn, before mourning two who had died in the action.

Saving one's brother was a remarkable act in that period. In England, the eldest child inherited the title, giving dynasties a good chance of a secure succession. But in Wales, all sons, of all ages, legitimate and illegitimate, could inherit. So Welsh princedoms were prone to be fragmented between warring brothers – a fatal weakness which the more unitary Norman conquerers exploited ruthlessly. They didn't have to divide and rule. The Welsh did the 'divide' bit for them. Among the Welsh, imprisoning one's siblings was common. Freeing them, and at personal risk, was much rarer. Owain, however, doesn't seem to have suffered by his fraternal generosity. He lived another forty-two years, passing the princedom peacefully to his son and retiring to the abbey of Ystrad Marchell (Strata Marcella) which he had founded.

One of the mainstays of Cymdeithas Owain Cyfeiliog in the 1970s and 1980s was Euros Bowen (1904-1988), regarded as one of the most important Welsh-language poets of the twentieth century.[26] He was a priest who served his first curacy in Wrexham before moving west, but who later retired to the town, where he had a family connection with the brewing trade. His poetry was dense and forbidding, pleasing highbrow critics almost as much as it repelled readers. I once slogged through his collected poems, hundreds of them, finding only one, 'Reredos', that I found even remotely satisfying. I mentioned this to a prominent Welsh scholar: 'Ah yes,' he said: 'That poem isn't typical of his work.' After Bowen's death, I found a stock of books from his personal library in a second-hand bookshop in one of Wrexham's arcades. They were signed, annotated, and some even contained relevant press cuttings he had carefully placed between the pages. I bought a couple, if only to give them a home.

Pen-y-Bryn has another literary connection too, although with a writer better-known for failure than success. James Beech was an eighteenth century wine merchant and minor poet remembered only for two things: having written a poem which attracted the ridicule of the great English man of letters Dr Samuel Johnson, and for having committed suicide in a particularly spectacular way – cutting his own throat so badly that he almost severed his head. In *Wrexham and its Neighbourhood*, in 1859, John Jones speculates as to whether the Pentice,[27] a seventeenth century building which stood almost directly opposite the Bowling Green public house, might have been Beech's House:

> A curious old house, in Pen-y-bryn, called the Pentice (from pent-house because it overhangs the street), was the residence, in the last century, of a literary gentleman; but whose name I have not learnt. He is said to have lived in great state; he dressed in black and wore a powdered wig, and when he walked out, carried a gold-headed cane, and was followed by a servant in livery. I conjecture that he must have been the Mr. Beech of whom we read in Boswell's life of Dr. Johnson.

Beech crops up twice in writings by or about Johnson. The Doctor himself mentions Beech in an article in the *Gentleman's Magazine* of June 1637, a month after the suicide, saying Beech was: "A Man of learning, great humanity and easy fortune, and was much respected but was blameable for his notions of religion, which 'tis thought were the occasion of his despair. He had an eloquent taste of poetry and has published some pieces which have been admired."[28] But they certainly hadn't been admired by Johnson. The careful praise he gives Beech following his death conceals the fact that Johnson had openly ridiculed him when he was alive.[29]

Johnson's faithful chronicler, James Boswell, records the incident in his *Life of Johnson*:

> Goldsmith produced some very absurd verses which had been pub-lickly recited to an audience for money. JOHNSON. 'I can match this nonsense. There was a poem called 'Eugenio', which came out some years ago, and concludes thus:
>
> > And now, ye trifling, self-assuming elves,
> > Brimful of pride, of nothing, of yourselves,
> > Survey Eugenio, view him o'er and o'er,
> > Then sink into yourselves, and be no more.

Boswell added a note:

> Mr Reed informs me that the Authour of 'Eugenio', Thomas Beech, a Wine Merchant at Wrexham in Denbighshire, soon after its publi-cation, viz. 17th May, 1737, cut his own throat... Johnson had read 'Eugenio' on his first coming to town.

An early or tragic death, preferably both, usually means a fast track to literary immortality, even for poets whose work contained more of promise than of achievement: Thomas Chatterton, for instance, or Rupert Brooke; or that other First World War casualty, the Trawsfynydd farmboy and posthumous eisteddfod-winner Hedd Wyn.[30] But a lasting memory requires a memorialiser, and Beech didn't have one. If Johnson had penned even a cursory elegy to Beech, the lesser poet would probably have got a plaque, a street name, maybe even a pub named after him. But it was his misfortune to be included in one of the classics of English literature only as a comic turn, and preserved to posterity as a buffoon. It's the kind of thing about which Doctor Johnson would perhaps have thrown off an epigram: better to be remembered as the butt of a great man's jest, than not be remembered at all. Perhaps.

Just round the corner is Tenters Square, named because textile-workers used the area for stretching and drying their cloth. In 1850, this became the site of Wrexham's second purpose-built jail, known as the Bridewell, a generic name for prisons, rather like the word 'Borstal', and taken from the name of a famous London Tudor prison. Wrexham Bridewell was eventually replaced by more mod-ern facilities, and by the 1980s, it was an empty, brooding relic eventually demolished to make way for modern housing, leaving only one of its outer walls standing. There was some demolition going on when I called by. A group of workers were removing an old garage building opposite the jail by *kicking* it down. They had tools, but were disdaining to use them, preferring instead to take it in turns to boot the walls down. Wrexham – the only town where using a crowbar or a sledgehammer might be seen to be a bit poofy.

Pen y Bryn – the Top of the Hill – has so far largely escaped the intense development which has affected that side of town, and it still provides a refuge for some of the more esoteric enterprises: a tattoo parlour, vintage clothes shop, Polish grocery, and the legendary Sergeant Peppers nightclub, one nightspot which has resisted the temptation to rename itself every couple of years – unlike its short-lived neighbour, Wrexham's first 'fun pub', Piggly Wiggly's. Pen y Bryn is a bit off-beat. A refuge for the quirky. But for how much longer, I don't know. The curving terrace of shops opposite the Albion Hotel once housed a fortune teller's premises, where I once saw a hand-written sign saying the office would be closed 'due to unforeseen circum-stances'. It doesn't take a fortune teller to say what fate is coming the way of Pen y Bryn, though. At the foot of the hill, Brook Street and the Gwenfro valley have been tamed by redevelopment, the river diverted, the brickwork repointed and the more tumbledown buildings removed like rotten teeth. The pavement at the bottom of Pen y Bryn has been relaid, inset with new steel-cased uplighters, like runway lights. All a bit twee for the kind of blokes who demolish buildings just by kicking them, but probably not too out of place on the way up to Fairy Road.

This side of town is fast changing. Brook Street and the Gwenfro valley area were long one of the town centre's more run-down areas, ever since the bus station was moved from there in the 1950s, taking the vital commercial footfall with it. The street did, however, retain one outstanding architectural feature, the Odeon cinema, built in art deco style in 1938 with cream-coloured tiled walls and a rectangular tower. It represented a newer age than that of the rival Hippodrome cinema in Henblas Street, built in unglamorous redbrick three decades before. But it was the Odeon which closed first. For years, its cinema showings had dwindled, the evenings being given over increasingly to bingo. Towards the end, the cinema showings finished midweek. I attended the very last one, on 15 May 1976, a showing of the Michael Caine / Sean Connery imperial India adventure *The Man Who Would be King*.[31] I was twelve, and already alert to the poignancy of the end of any era, whether of the British Empire or the empire of

Oscar Deutsch, Entertainer Of Nations. But there was no ceremony that night, no announcement, and no audience to speak of. The credits rolled, the curtains slid together, and that was it. Film made its exit, bingo flowed into the vacuum. By now, bingo too has called its final eyes-down. The building is now the Liquid nightclub.

Liquid is something Wrexham town centre knows all about, not only in the consumption of it in the pubs, bars and nightclubs, but also in the subsequent expulsion of it, against walls and in shop doorways. With up to ten thousand regular drinkers in the town, it got so bad the council installed open-air urinals on the corner of Brook Street and Town Hill, modesty giving way to expediency in the interests of getting the pee into the drains not the doorways. They borrowed the idea from France. Don't let anyone tell you that Wrexham doesn't have a Continental air. We might not do pavement cafés like the French, we might not do fashion or food like the French – but one thing's for sure, we can certainly pee like the French.

Development has transformed this side of town. The once-derelict Island Green brewery, its two adjacent malthouses like an upturned brassiere in scalloped slate, has been given a residential makeover. The Old Three Tuns pub, with its distinctive blue-and-white relief sculpted gable, has been renovated too. And the new Island Green shopping centre has turned the former Central Station site from a makeshift pot-holed car park into a white-pillared compound of chain-stores, where the produce of the furthest-flung corners of commerce's global empire is offered at permanent never-to-be-repeated discounts.

Not so long ago, before the economic flow reversed like an electric

circuit, this town was an exporter. Coal. Steel. Beer. From Wrexham to the world. And not just material goods. The massive rectangular church, dominating the skyline like a perpendicular power station, wasn't there just to store spiritual energy for the benefit of the parish; it was there to send it out along the gridlines of the British Empire to brighten the darkest corners of the world with the light of Christianity.

At least, that's how the popular nineteenth century preacher and hymnwriter Bishop Reginald Heber[32] saw it when he came to Wrexham in 1819 to visit his father-in-law, the rector. Heber had been asked to preach at St Giles' on missionary work. The night before the service, Heber wrote a poem, 'From Greenland's Icy Mountains', dashing it off in twenty minutes while sitting in the drawing room with his friends. In it, he envisaged "benighted" people in remote countries crying out for salvation: "They call us to deliver / Their land from error's chain." It was sung in St Giles' the following morning, and became the most famous missionary hymn in the English-speaking world. In the second verse, Heber depicts a tropical paradise where "The heathen in his blindness / Bows down to wood and stone."[33]

Nearly eighty years later, with the British Empire at the height of its power, Rudyard Kipling adapted the lines for a wry comment on the empire's attitudes to its subject peoples, put into the mouth of a Cockney soldier in India:

> The 'eathen in 'is blindness bows down to wood an' stone;
> 'E don't obey no orders unless they is 'is own;
> 'E keeps 'is side-arms awful: 'e leaves 'em all about,
> An' then comes up the regiment an' pokes the 'eathen out. [34]

By the time that poem appeared, in 1896, Heber had been buried for seventy years in the earth of the India he'd depicted in the poem. He'd followed his own advice and had gone, a missionary bishop, to Calcutta in 1823, dying there three years later, at the age of forty-three.

In 1926, a hundred years after Heber's death, a grey plaque was erected in Wrexham to record where the poem was written. They put it high on the stone walls of Vicarage Hill, as close as possible to where the old vicarage used to stand. The poem is still there, but you won't find it in the hymn books any more. All that talk of heathens and 'error's chain' isn't politically correct. The site of the vicarage is now a chain store, most of whose goods are made cheaply in the countries to which Heber wanted to bring 'the lamp of life,' Exploit them, yes. Insult them, no. Progress.

RHOSDDU

'Hello. I'm looking for Roz's do.' The driver had wound down his window to ask me for directions. He was being a bit specific though. Roz's do. Who was Roz? And where might she be having her do? Wrexham was a big place. I could hardly be expected to know the location of every social function. 'Have you got an address?' I asked him. 'Yes,' he said, looking harrassed, and showing me a piece of paper. 'Roz Do.' I looked at the piece of paper he showed me. 'Ah! Rhosddu.' I was able to tell him he was already in the right part of town. He drove off looking only slightly relieved.

Until the railway age, Rhosddu – the name means 'black moor' – was a boggy area on the outskirts of Wrexham, crossed by a causeway. When the railway came, in the mid nineteenth century, and a goods yard was established nearby, the area was drained and developed for houses. The opening of Acton Colliery fuelled the growth further.[35] The area housed many miners: seventeen of those killed in the Gresford mining disaster came from Rhosddu. Now it's a quiet area of redbrick streets close to the town centre, with the usual collection of pharmacists, hairdressers and corner shops.

One corner shop particularly stood out. On the pavement is a sign advertising Limpopo Foods. This used to be the old Rhosddu post office. Now it's packed with African goods. The shopkeeper, Bafana Ndlovu, arrived in Wrexham from Zimbabwe five years ago. I ask him how Wrexham compares with other places in the UK. He says he can't tell me, as he'd come straight to Wrexham and hadn't lived anywhere else. His clientele are mainly from southern Africa, although

he's also started stocking goods for West Africans, Ghanaians and Nigerians, too. We chat about South Africa, where I'd been lecturing about six months previously. While I was there, the news bulletins had been filled with stories about refugees from Zimbabwe flooding the border posts. He nods; he keeps in touch with news from home over the internet. I have a look around the shop, toying briefly with

the idea of buying some biltong. There would be something so Wilbur Smith about that. Instant nutritional machismo. But this is Rhosddu not Rhodesia, so I end up buying a PS chocolate bar made by Cadbury of South Africa. It turns out to be white chocolate and, even for my sweet tooth, a touch too sweet. I should have gone for the biltong; I feel as if I've failed some obscure test of manhood.

A few yards further down is a little park formed from the old Dissenters' Burial Ground. In the middle of it stands an obelisk memorial to Morgan Llwyd, the puritan divine who spent much of his career in Wrexham. Ysgol Morgan Llwyd was named after him when it opened in 1963, although I managed to spend five years there without having a clue who Morgan Llwyd was. It was only many years later, when researching Welsh mysticism, that I encountered his work.

Llwyd was born in Meirionnydd in 1619, and educated in Wrexham from the age of ten. His grandfather, Huw Llwyd, had been an astrologer and magician, but Morgan chose a less arcane spiritual path, converting to Christianity in Wrexham, becoming a Puritan and serving as a Parliamentary army chaplain in the Civil War. Afterwards, he settled in Wrexham, at Brynyffynnon, working as a preacher and minister. He wrote eleven books, eight Welsh, three English, all religious. His best-known is perhaps *Llyfr y Tri Aderyn*, the 'Book of the Three Birds', a fable in which the creatures of the book's title discuss religious subjects. Innovative at the time; heavy going now. Much of his work was aimed at preparing the Welsh for the Second Coming, which he thought imminent. Llwyd himself died in 1659, and awaits the Second Coming in Rhosddu, although the exact site of his grave isn't known, as the headstones have been cleared and placed around the walls of the park. The memorial simply marks the fact that he's in there somewhere.

Another hundred yards or so down Rhosddu Road is the junction with Spring Road. Here, at number six, a plaque marks the birthplace of the racing driver John Godfrey Parry-Thomas, who briefly held the world land speed record in 1926, and who was killed while trying to regain it in 1927. He was born on 6 April 1884, the second son of the curate of St James Church, Rhosddu, the Rev. John William Thomas, and he was brought up here until he was five, when the family moved to the Oswestry area.[36] After a career in engineering, he became a professional racing driver and gradually became drawn into the high-octane world of record attempts, finally assembling a car of his own which was capable of trying for the record. He bought the car from the estate of Count Louis Vorrow Zborowski, who had been killed in a crash in the Italian Grand Prix at Monza in 1924. The vehicle's fateful origins didn't worry Parry-Thomas. He fitted her out with a 27,059cc Liberty aeroplane engine, a Benz gearbox, Leyland steering, and a chassis made by Rubery Owen of the Midlands;[37] he streamlined the body, and he called her 'Babs'. Then, with the sponsorship of Shell Mex, he took her down to south west Wales to a long stretch of featureless sand called Pendine.

Pendine was the Cape Canaveral of its day: a magnet for the highest achievements of engineering, ingenuity and adventure, and a place which held the attention of the world as men pushed machines faster than they had ever gone before. The land speed record had been set here in September 1924 when Malcolm Campbell's Bluebird reached a hundred and forty-six miles per hour. And Campbell had raised the stakes even higher in the same place in July of the following year, when he reached a hundred and fifty miles per hour. This was what Parry-Thomas had to beat.

He more than beat it. He smashed it. On April 27, 1926, Babs reached 168 miles per hour. And on the following day, he broke his own record, and set the bar at 171.02 mph. He'd added thirteen per

cent to Campbell's record speed, and Parry-Thomas was now officially the fastest man in the world. Campbell congratulated him, and then set to work preparing Bluebird to get the record back. He did it less than a year later, in January 1927, recording 174mph at Pendine, only three miles per hour faster than Parry-Thomas, but enough. Now the pressure was back on Parry-Thomas.

On 3 March 1927, he took Babs down to Pendine again. He had flu, but record attempts were costly affairs and couldn't be postponed lightly. He took off on a timed run. He was just one second short of his own previous record time when Babs' chain drive snapped, decapitating him. The car skidded, cartwheeled, crashed and burned. Parry-Thomas' crew, who raced to the crash site, had to break his legs to get his body out of the wreckage before the fire consumed it.

John Godfrey Parry-Thomas was buried in Surrey. Babs was buried where she lay, an invisible memorial to her driver, and also to Pendine's history as a record-attempt course. Whether because of the sense of ill-omen, or, more likely, because of the unreliable Welsh weather conditions, the focus for the record attempt moved to the salt flats of the United States. Pendine was the last place in Europe where the land speed record was set, and Parry-Thomas was the last man to die in the attempt. The world moved on, more records were made and broken, and Babs stayed where she was.

At least, she stayed there for forty years, after which Owen Wyn Owen, an engineering lecturer from north Wales, defied the misgivings of locals and historians and got permission to have her exhumed from the site, which was by then a Ministry of Defence missile-testing range. For years, he restored her, painstakingly. Now, pristine again, she leads a double life, spending the winter in the National Museum of Wales, and the summer at the specially-built Museum of Speed overlooking the sands.

It was a brooding day when I visited the place where the son of the curate of Rhosddu sped into eternity. The country was being lashed by vicious January storms in which a number of people had been killed by floods, flying debris, and falling trees. The death toll increased with every hourly update on the car radio. It had reached eleven as I caught the four o'clock bulletin as I drove down the steep hill into Pendine through the narrow lanes and the bare swaying tree branches. The light was already failing. And in case the brakes failed too, the hill has several escape lanes, a measure taken to prevent the kind of accident which befell a bus driver who was killed here in 1977 when his vehicle's brakes let him down. Pendine doesn't take accidents lightly, as I was to find out.

Pendine itself is a strangely scattered little collection of chip-shops, bungalows, restaurants, surf-shops, static caravans and pubs, looking as if it's been collected from spare components salvaged from other seaside settlements and reassembled here on any spare bit of land available, but never quite gelling. Any temporary coherence it might acquire from summer activity was certainly absent on this bleak late afternoon. Mine was the only car in the partially-flooded seafront car park next to the Museum of Speed, and there was only one other human being in sight: an anoraked man up on the seafront, pulling a disconsolate terrier through the squalls of rain.

The museum itself was closed for the winter months. Built in 1996, it's a small modern building with a curved art-deco-style window facing the sands where the fateful record attempt happened. I looked through the glass into the darkened interior. It was empty except for the skeletal outlines of two vintage motorcycles, waiting like metal handmaidens either side of the central space where the resurrected goddess of speed is enthroned for half a year, a petroleum Persephone, returning to her kingdom with the sun.

There wasn't any sun in evidence this afternoon. Nor much sand either, for that matter. The waves were clawing at the sea-wall, each surge only a few feet away from adding to that day's body count. But no careless walker along the storm-threatened path could claim they hadn't been warned of the danger. There were warning signs of every conceivable size and shape. Whether it's because of the place's history or just because of a peculiar sense of apprehension on the part of the local authorities, but I have never seen so many cautions and admonitions. In the fifty or so yards around the Museum of Speed, there was a fluorescent grove of ominous symbols warning against events ranging from the blindingly obvious to the freakishly unlikely.

Among this silent forest of foreboding was a harmless-looking telegraph pole, one of millions of similar ones which stand around the country, unremarked and unguarded. But here, a yellow sign warned of electrocution and showed a lurid image of a human figure being struck down by a jagged thunderbolt as if he were the victim of an angry god.

Clearly, in Pendine, they have no intention of letting lightning strike in the same place twice. I got back in the car and drove, cautiously, into the deserted main street, and climbed the hill out of the village. I passed the welcome sign. 'Pendine' it said. 'Please drive carefully.' Underneath another sign warned 'Speed Cameras'

ACTON AND GARDEN VILLAGE

The road out of Wrexham back towards Chester leads through Acton, one of the town's leafier and more comfortable suburbs. As befits an area which was once the centre of the short-lived Welsh diamond industry.

The diamonds weren't Welsh, of course. There may be small amounts of gold in those hills to the west, but no-one's found diamonds yet. No, the rocks were brought here by Sir Bernard Oppenheimer, a diamond merchant from Belgium who bought the Acton Park estate in 1917 from the Cunliffe family, who had held it for over a hundred years. He opened a diamond-polishing factory there, employing disabled ex-servicemen, of whom there were many in those years of the Great War.[38] But an enterprise which might have put Wrexham on the world jewellery map came to a premature end when Sir Bernard died suddenly in 1923.

Acton Hall was once Wrexham's capitol, the chief house of the district. It was home, from the seventeenth century, to the influential Jeffreys family, who counted among their number the notorious 'Judge Jeffreys'. Born George Jeffreys at Acton Hall in 1645, he followed family tradition and became a lawyer – the kind who gives lawyers a bad name: boozy, bad-tempered and ruthlessly ambitious. When he became Chief Justice of Chester Circuit in 1680, Charles the Second called him "the worst that ever disgraced the bench" and added: "He has no learning, no sense, no manners and has more impudence than ten street walkers."[39] But the king, a survivor himself, knew another survivor when he saw one, and in 1683, he made Jeffreys Lord Chief Justice. Jeffreys repaid the royal patronage with interest two years later when, after the death of Charles, Protestants led by the Duke of Monmouth rebelled against the late monarch's Roman Catholic brother James, who had become king. The rebels were defeated at the battle of Sedgemoor in Somerset, and thirteen hundred of them were then tried at Taunton for treason. Jeffreys presided. In a worse temper than ever – due to agonising kidney stones, his biographers speculate – he didn't waste time on niceties like a fair trial. Or even an *un*fair trial. He offered the rebels a pardon if they pleaded guilty. And when they did so, he hanged them – over three hundred of them. And he had another eight hundred transported into slavery.

Although a Protestant himself, Jeffreys hoped his zeal in the royal cause would secure further patronage. And when James rewarded him by making him Lord Chancellor, he must have thought he'd made the right choice. But he was wrong. Three years later he was a fugitive himself, trying to flee the country disguised as a sailor after his royal Catholic patron had been the target of another rebellion, this time a successful one which placed the Protestant William and Mary on the throne. Jeffreys was caught and put into protective custody in the Tower of London, where he died in 1689.[40]

As the birthplace of a historical figure like that, you might think Acton Hall would have been preserved as a showpiece tourist attraction. And people certainly suggested that it should be saved when, after spells as an army camp, a school, a council office and a furniture store, it was slated for demolition in the 1950s. *The Encyclopaedia of Wrexham* notes the official report which recommended the house be razed: "Without being anxious to betray ignorance, we should like you to tell us one feature either of architectural or historic interest possessed by Acton Hall... Please do not think us Philistines – we are not."[41] The report warned darkly that the building could attract 'juvenile delinquents'. So that settles it then. The council duly had it demolished and put a rubbish dump there instead. All that remains is the grand gateway to the park, topped with four sculpted greyhounds, a feature which gave its name to the pub built there in the 1970s, the Four Dogs. Please do not think us Philistines – we are not.

If the way it dealt with Acton Hall was lacking, Wrexham Council had more cause for pride in the way it provided social housing. The Garden Village it built on part of the Acton Park estate during the First World War was the first in Wales and is still a model of its kind, spacious, well-proportioned, with plenty of facilities: shops, school, chapel, sports fields. It was built for the miners and managers of the new Gresford Colliery which was being opened just outside the town. And it was an instant success, marking a huge step forward for the welfare of mining families. But less than two decades after it was built, the lives of its inhabitants were to be overshadowed by a communal tragedy, one for which better housing conditions were no compensation.

notes

1. Dodd, *op. cit.*, p18.
2. Wrexham's few planned streets such as Grosvenor Road and King Street have been fragmented
3. W. Alister Williams, *The Encyclopaedia of Wrexham*, (Bridge Books, 2001), p207.
4. *Ibid*, p202.
5. *Ibid*, p31.
6. *Ibid*, p13.
7. The oldest licensed premises in Wrexham is the Bowling Green pub at Pen y Bryn, dating back to 1802. *Ibid*, p49.
8. Dodd *op. cit.*, p96.
9. http://knowhere.co.uk/3265_eatdrink.html
10. Brewing and breweries:
    http://www.bbc.co.uk/wales/northeast/sites/wrexham/pages/wrexham12.shtml
    History of Wrexham Lager:
    http://www.wrexham.gov.uk/english/heritage/brewery_tour/lager_brewery.htm
    History of Border Brewery:
    http://www.wrexham.gov.uk/english/heritage/brewery_tour/soames_brewery.htm
    Bernard Asquith, former Wrexham Lager employee, gives a short history of the brew ery: http://www.bbc.co.uk/wales/northeast/sites/wrexham/pages/lager.shtml
11. Television journalist Peter Sissons is descended from brewer William Sissons, of the Cambrian Brewery. Williams, *op. cit.*, p337.
12. There was a short-lived Austro-Bavarian brewery in Tottenham between 1881 and 1894. Williams *op. cit.*, p336.
13. Opposite, in Union Street, a plaque marks the house where Edwin Hughes was born, in 1830. As a trooper in the 13th Light Dragoons, he took part in the Charge of the Light Brigade at Balaclava in 1854. Afterwards, he enjoyed lifelong celebrity as 'Balaclava Ned', and in 1923 became the last survivor of the charge. He died, eventually, in 1927, aged ninety-seven.
14. John Simons Funfairs: http://www.johnsimonsfunfairs.com/simons_family.htm
15. A family legend tells how my great-grandfather, Heth Jones, was in demand here as a judge of animals, with both vendors and purchasers deferring to his opinion.
16. Williams *op. cit.*, p157.
17. In the 1990s, it moved to the old Cartrefle college site, where it has since expanded.
18. Williams *op. cit.*, p256.
19. Nixon's ancestors in Caia Park:
    http://news.bbc.co.uk/1/hi/wales/north_east/4076854.stm
20 'Eira yn Wrecsam', *Lleoedd*, (Barddas, 1984), p13.
21. Office of Population Censuses and Surveys, 2001 Census. Table UV64 Welsh Language Skills.
22. 'Sbwriel', Ed. Aled Lewis Evans, *Cerddi Clwyd*, (Gomer, 2004), p66.
23. Messages taken from the fund-raising commemorative bricks which fans paid to have installed in the wall of the Pryce Griffiths stand. Here, grouped roughly according to theme, and with personal names removed.
24. And since to 11/12 Neptune Court, Vanguard Way, Cardiff.
25. See Ed. Thomas Parry, *The Oxford Book of Welsh Verse*, (OUP, 1962)
26. Euros Bowen:
    www.bbc.co.uk/cymru/gogleddddwyrain/enwogion/llen/pages/euros_bowen.shtml
27. Demolished in about 1890, Williams *op.cit.*, p240.
28. *Ibid*, p38.

29. Doctor Johnson visited Wrexham on 6 September 1774. His comments, recorded in his journal, *A Journey into North Wales in the Year 1774*, are brief: "We lay at Wrexham; a busy, extensive, and well built town. It has a very large and magnificent Church. It has a famous fair."
30. Ellis Humphrey Evans (1887-1817) joined the Royal Welch Fusiliers at Wrexham Barracks, went to the Western Front and died in the battle of Pilkem Ridge, Belgium, on 31 July 1917.
31. Date from Williams *op. cit.*, p228.
32. His dates are 1783-1826. *ibid*, p162.
33. Heber originally wrote 'savage', but then toned it down a bit to 'heathen'.
34. 'The 'Eathen', *Barrack Room Ballads* (1896).
35. Williams *op. cit.*, p262.
36. *Ibid*, p236.
37. Founded by Alfred Ernest Owen of Wrexham, former partner in Wrexham's Rogers and Jackson company who'd moved to make his fortune in engineering in the English Midlands, *Ibid*, p276.
38. *Ibid*, p230.
39. Details from Wrexham CBC website.
40. Williams, p182 Wrexham CBC website: www.wrexham.gov.uk/english/heritage/foster_cunliffe_appeal/painting/acton_park.htm
41. *Ibid*, p22.

North

GRESFORD

The village of Gresford had been immortalised in the rhyme about the
Seven Wonders of Wales long before it acquired a darker distinction.
The list of 'wonders' included the peal of bells in the church, which is
a fine perpendicular fifteenth century structure built in the distinctive
honey-coloured 'Cefn' stone of the Maelor district, on the wide terrace
of land between Wrexham and the Cheshire plain. With its village
green and cottages, Gresford could look like the stuff of a rural idyll.
Church, chimes and children's voices. But appearances can mislead. If
you know what's under the surface, then you know that this is actually
Wrexham's saddest place.

The clue was always there. This is an old settlement. One of the yew
trees in the churchyard is fifteen hundred years old, dating from the
time before the Saxons arrived, conquered the area and gave it the
name it bears today. Yew trees were sacred to the Celts, so the site had
clearly been a place of devotion long before the Saxons came. Just how
long became apparent in 1908, when a Roman altar was discovered in
the church. It was dedicated to Nemesis, the ancient goddess of fate.
She was the daughter of Erebus, the king of the underworld, and his
sister Nyx, the goddess of the night. And she was the granddaughter
of Chaos. One of her names meant 'the one from whom there is no
escape.' Remorseless and implacable, her name is still used to mean
one's worst enemy.

In the same year that the altar of Nemesis was found in the church,
the task of sinking a shaft into the dark underworld beneath the village
was finished, and Gresford Colliery was ready to start work.

In a short while, there were hundreds of men working underground there. And by 1934, the workforce had grown to 2200, drawn
not only from nearby Garden Village which was built especially for
the workers, but from many of the other surrounding villages too:
Brymbo, Brynteg, Coedpoeth, Minera, Rhos, Southsea, Broughton,
Summerhill, Gwersyllt, Llay. Which meant that the whole area felt the
shock when the miners' nemesis finally struck.

On 22 September 1934, there were more than five hundred men
working the night shift in the colliery. That was a higher number than
usual, as many were working an extra shift in order to have the following day off to watch the local derby match between Wrexham and
Tranmere. At eight minutes past two in the morning, a spark ignited
a build-up of gas, and a devastating explosion ripped through the
Dennis section of the mine. Of the men working in the Dennis, only

six escaped. The rest – two hundred and sixty-one of them – were killed. Miners and rescue workers tried to reach the area to look for survivors, but the fire was uncontrollable, and three of the rescuers were killed too. They had no option other than to seal off the whole section, and leave their comrades there in one mass grave, two thousand feet under the surface.[1] It was the second-worst mining disaster in Welsh his-

tory,[2] and the last mining disaster of that scale in Britain ever.

There were hardship appeals, of course, and a trial of some of the managers. They were fined a total of £140 with £350 costs. Less than two pounds for every life lost. Six months later, the mine was back in production, and within a couple of years its workforce was almost as big as at the time of the disaster. It continued in production until 1974, when it closed due to geological difficulties. The pithead winding gear remained, like a skeletal headstone to the entombed workers below.

But it didn't remain very long. Despite outraged protests, Wrexham Council had it demolished. It would cost too much trouble to keep repainting it, they said. They saved only the pitwheel which they tucked away in a little memorial garden next to the social club in the corner of the new industrial estate. Please do not think us Philistines – we are not. When the Prince of Wales came to open it in 1982, councillors and dignitaries thronged the special marquee. Survivors of the disaster and widows and children of the victims were kept behind the ropes outside. Nemesis must have been looking away.

I visited the site in company with Tom Ellis, the former Wrexham MP, ex-miner and ex-colliery manager, whose father had been one of the rescue brigade during the disaster. He remembers his father being called out that Saturday morning, and he recalls that it was on his advice that the pit was sealed and the attempt to recover the bodies abandoned. He recalls too, when, as an MP and with a long career in the mining industry behind him, he tried, unsuccessfully, to persuade the council to keep the winding gear. His father, who had risked his life during the rescue attempt, didn't even get an invitation to the unveiling.

There's a packaging factory on the site of the colliery buildings, now. And the memorial itself stands next to the Gresford Colliery Social Club. Tetley's Bitter. Strictly No Parking. Reserved for Chairman. On one side is a guilty-looking playing field, with a scorched bonfire patch, old pallets, and some roomless plastic chairs. A sign warns: No Tipping of Bonfire Material on this Premises. The site is in the angle of the by-pass and the road to Chester, an area of high vehicle traffic. The monument shares the space with Charlie's Hand Car Wash. Plastic bumper shine £2.50. Interior leather care £15. Don't forget to ask for a loyalty card.

It's hard to believe that Gresford is a mining village, and one with such a tragic history. It should have gloomy terraces punctuated by stark, unadorned chapels. Instead it looks like one of the idealised pictures of a rural village that were used in the 1960s to advertise National Savings. As safe as houses. Just outside the village, it even has its own boating lake, Gresford Flash, a ten acre natural lake with one of Britain's smallest sailing clubs, and a variety of birdlife that keeps the twitchers' binoculars busy year-round. Even on the fringes of the town, within sound of the bypass, nature thrives. And even on the fringes of the town, places can still feel isolated.

They felt a lot more isolated two hundred years ago, before tarmac and streetlights, when the Gresford Wolfman was on the prowl.

I had to do a double-take when I came across this story in Cledwyn Fychan's *Galwad y Blaidd* (Call of the Wolf)[3], his masterly study of the natural – and unnatural – history of the wolf in Wales. A wolfman in Wrexham? And not in some fabled medieval past, but in 1791, the period of the French Revolution, the year William Pitt was British Prime Minister and George Washington the American President. Surely wolfmen belong in some pre-modern mythological age? But it turns out that the Gresford case is well-documented, although not well-explained, as wolves had been extinct for two hundred years in Wales when it happened.

It began in 1790, when a creature described as part man and part wolf attacked the horses of the stage coach between Denbigh and Wrexham. Then in 1791, a Gresford farmer came face-to-face with the creature when it killed his dog in front of him, and he had to barricade himself in his cottage while the creature killed and mutilated his stock outside. There was a sequel seven years later, ten miles to the east, at Bickerton in Cheshire, where two travellers saw a wolf-like shape on a ridge and heard its howling. A search the following day came across the mutilated bodies of two tramps in a forest. Shortly afterwards, a local minister received a letter saying the creature was the ghost of a man burned at the stake by villagers in 1400 and that the only way to be rid of it was to paint crosses on all the houses in the parish. Cledwyn Fychan speculates that this might have been done, as no more was seen or heard of the wolfman.

But there are indeed crosses built into the walls of many of the houses at Marford, at the base of the escarpment where the road from Gresford angles down to the plain. The village is a collection of ornate Gothic-style cottages built in the late eighteenth and early nineteenth century by the estate of nearby Trevalyn Hall. So the period would coincide with that of the wolfman story. Or maybe, of course, the crosses were just innocent decoration, and the wolfman story was invented to explain them.

This road used to be the main route from Wrexham to Chester. But now, most of the heavy traffic is carried by the new bypass running on a roughly parallel, but straighter, route, just to the north west. As a result, the string of villages on the remaining couple of miles of the old road to the English border have recovered something of their rural character. Rossett, with its half-timbered watermill, looks like something out of a Constable painting. There's no doubt that you're in the country. There's a smell of fresh manure. A sign in a shop window invites: 'Come and see the new-born lambs! All proceeds to Church funds'. There's a mud-spattered Land Rover outside the convenience store. Many of the other cars in the street are four-by-fours.

The village's Welsh name, probably originally 'Yr Orsedd Goch,' 'The Red Throne', has long ago been streamlined to 'Rossett.' Welsh made easy. None of those troublesome rolled 'r's or throat-scraping 'ch's. The border is within a stone's throw here. Skies are broad, horizons wide. A foundation stone of the Presbyterian Chapel in the main street shows that it was laid in 1875 by Dwight L. Moody, the great American preacher. With the composer and singer Ira Sankey, he was one half of 'Moody and Sankey', the Tim Rice and Andrew Lloyd Webber of nineteenth century Christianity. He made his visit

to Rossett during a tour of Britain in which crowds numbering up to twenty thousand gathered to hear him speak.

The village noticeboard has a helpful guide to local features and history. Marford Mill was mentioned in the Domesday Book in 1086. Trevalyn Hall was built in 1576. The village green used to be called 'The Plantation'; "Gypsies camped there and roasted hedgehogs". I wonder if the gypsies did anything else while they were there. They can't have roasted hedgehogs *all* the time; the enjoyment must have worn off after a while. Then I notice another entry. 'Almere Ferry'. Apparently, it was used by the Duke of Westminster's gamekeeper to patrol for poachers, and also to ferry seasonal crop pickers across from Cheshire. A ferry across the river Dee, deep inland between England and Wales, formerly used by cross-border gangmasters. I had to see it.

It took two attempts. On the first occasion, following a few days' heavy rain, I found the road marked by one of those temporary roadsigns warning of a flood. I ignored the sign, reasoning that floods usually recede pretty quickly and that council workmen probably leave the warnings there for longer than strictly necessary. Wrong. A few bends further down the road, and the car was on the verge not of some bracing three-second splash, and a quick flick of the wipers, but of a sheet of water stretching to the horizon. The road ran into the water like a lifeboat's slipway. A little further ahead, a green-wellied family were carrying a rowing boat between the hedges. They were just too far away for me to call to them. So I watched them carry the boat until the water was deep enough for it to float. Then they got in and rowed quietly away up the lane into

the distance. I climbed to the top of the floodgate. For miles eastward, the fields were square silver pools in the dark frames of the bare hedges. In the hundreds of acres of water, a few farms stood on their green rises of land like islands.

Several cars were parked by the floodgates. Several boats lay there too, waiting to be used in this informal inland ferry service. Park and Row. Driving back, I passed a local woman walking her dog, and asked her about it. She pointed out that nearly all the houses had small boats outside in their gardens. They did too. The whole area flooded badly in 2000, she said. The floodgate I'd climbed was part of the Environment Agency's response. It meant people to the west of it were unlikely to suffer again if the Dee overflowed, but those living to the east had to transfer

to boats once the cars reached the water's edge. I was glad I'd made the trip here. This was a different Wrexham to any I had imagined. A Wrexham where people keep rowing boats in their gardens like other people might keep lawnmowers.

But, lacking a boat of my own, I hadn't been able to get to Almere Ferry itself. Which was clearly now a necessity. A few weeks later, the waters having receded, I did get there. Almere Ferry is where the Alyn river flows into the Dee, and where the meander of the river has isolated a little loop of land on the Welsh bank. The road is a raised causeway, and the land on either side is a green and greedy-looking swamp which looks ready to swallow your car up to the wheel arches. A sign warns that the site belongs to Warrington Anglers Association. It's an angler's colony: a circular laager of static caravans and wooden cabins, gimcrack compounds with lanterns, pub signs, and nautical paraphernalia, each with its own boat. Surely the strangest settlement in the borough. Wrexham on Sea. Or Wrexham on River, anyway, which is only slightly less weird.

GWERSYLLT AND DISTRICT

Dave Cooke is wearing the watch Vladimir Putin, the President of Russia, gave him.

"Can I touch it?" I ask.

"Sure," he says, stretching his brawny arm across the desk.

I touch it. A twenty-four carat piece of history.

We're talking in his office at his home in Rhosrobin, one of several suburbs to the north of Wrexham. Like neighbouring Bradley and Gwersyllt, this village is a quiet and unassuming place. It certainly doesn't look like the birthplace and headquarters of a global aid agency. But there are plenty of clues on the office walls: testimonials in backwards writing from Eastern European countries, and gifts from grateful communities from the Baltic to the Black Sea. I'm more impressed than Dave Cooke seems to be. He doesn't keep doing what he does for the kudos. He does it for the kids.

It was in 1990 that it all started. Dave and his friends John and Carol Roberts were having a meal at the house when the television news began showing the harrowing scenes in Romanian orphanages, as the plight of that country's abandoned children first started to come to light at the end of the Ceausescu regime. He knew he had to do something. He and John decided they'd drive out a lorry full of supplies.

The next morning, he recruited his brother Paul and his friend Dai Hughes, who decided to publicise the venture on the radio station for which he worked, Marcher Sound, based a short distance away at Mold Road in Gwersyllt. In no time, donations were flooding in from all over north Wales and north west England: food, clothes, medical supplies, X-ray machines, wheelchairs and incubators. Dave had planned to take two lorries. But the project grew, and seven trucks eventually made the gruelling journey from north Wales to Eastern Europe. Dave's eight-year-old daughter Naomi supplied the logo, a yellow Christmas star. His sister Jan had the idea of asking local children to fill a shoebox full of gifts for the children in Romania. It was an instant success. Operation Christmas Child was born.

Since then, the charity has grown every year, both in the number of boxes sent and the number of countries concerned; millions of boxes have now been sent worldwide by road and by giant chartered Antonov 124 cargo aircraft. Worldwide, there are three hundred people managing the work, and the annual turnover is in the millions of dollars. 'Dollars' because in 1995 OCC became part of Samaritan's Purse International, an American evangelical aid organisation run by

Franklin Graham, son of the evangelist Billy Graham.[4]

That caused controversy, because, while Dave Cooke and his partners had never hidden their Christian motives for their humanitarian work, the Americans made it much more explicit, giving out evangelistic leaflets with the boxes, leading to accusations that they were using charity as a means of spreading the gospel. The dispute rumbles on; the *Guardian* fulminates, the Humanist Association complains, the United Nations criticise, other aid organisations distance themselves.[5] Dave Cooke himself, who has since moved on from OCC, thinks the Americans developed the evangelistic side 'maybe a bit too much'. But the shoeboxes keep coming in, and keep being shipped out, as many as ever. Whatever the rights and wrongs of the evangelistic enterprise which OCC has now become, that meeting in Rhosrobin created an organisation that has become part of the experience of millions of people, and which made Wrexham the centre of a huge web of worldwide activity.

But not for much longer. Samaritan's Purse are centralising their UK work and are closing the depot on Wrexham Industrial Estate from which OCC has operated since its earliest days. Dave Cooke drives me over there to see the last supplies before they're moved out. The warehouse is half-empty, and there are only a couple of workers left, tying up the loose ends before the work moves over the border. Boxes marked 'Wrexham to Liberia' are stacked ceiling-high. There are brand-new bicycles, toys, and thousands upon thousands of shoeboxes. There's a trophy cabinet with the gifts given by grateful municipalities. One of them is a graceful carved wolf. 'From Beslan,' Dave tells me. He was there in the wake of the massacre. His new charity, Teams4U, does team-building work in the world's trouble spots: Rwanda, Uganda, Liberia. Other gifts are from places where Dave and his charity have helped in the orphanages.

I've seen the suffering in the Romanian orphanages too. I went there with a relief convoy in 1991. Hospitals with empty medicine cabinets and with urine from open toilets running down the stairs. Orphanages where the children were swaddled in tight bedclothes and put to sleep in stifling rooms for twenty-three hours a day, woken only to be fed, changed and wrapped up again to sleep their childhood away. Institutions where the workers refuse to give the children toys, 'because it makes them lively'. I saw it, but I knew I lacked the heart to try to fix it. Report on it, yes, I could do that. Give money, too. Or fill shoeboxes, if it comes to that. But the hands-on, face-to-face work, that's for other people. People who seem to have a source of human compassion to which I don't have access. Or is it just human compassion?

I ask Dave if he's doing what he's doing because he's religious. He doesn't like that word. Too 'namby-pamby'. He's a Christian. He's trying to follow Jesus' example. What church does he attend? He tells me of a small local congregation of which he's a member. What denomination is that? I ask him; the demarcations between different brands of religion fascinate me. But Dave has to think before answering. Denominations don't mean much to him. The children do.

As I leave, I notice that his house is called 'Cair Paravel', the name of the castle in *The Chronicles of Narnia*, by C.S. Lewis, the great Christian author. From somewhere in my memory I dredge up the fact that C.S. Lewis' family came from Caergwrle, only a couple of miles away, over the Flintshire border. Dave's intrigued, so I offer to try to find out exactly where Lewis' ancestors lived.

It was more difficult than I thought. Lewis' great-great-grandfather, Richard Lewis, was born in Caergwrle, as was his great-grandfather, Joseph, a churchman turned Methodist minister, who moved to Saltney on Deeside, where the family had connections with the boilermaking trade in Liverpool's shipping industry. It was that industry which took Joseph's son, Richard, to Ireland, where *his* son, Albert, was born, and where, in due course, his grandson, Clive Staples Lewis, came into the world, in Belfast, in 1898.[6] The family valued their Welsh ancestry. C.S. Lewis himself claimed to be more Welsh than Irish, and he must have had at least some acquaintance with the Welsh language: he adapted the word *caer*, meaning 'castle', for the name of his own mythical Narnian fortress, and he was also, in later life, a great friend of J.R.R. Tolkien, of *Lord of the Rings* fame. Tolkien could read Welsh and used it as the partial basis for some of his invented Elvish languages.

A redbrick house on Deeside, Number Five, Watkin Street, Sandycroft, is the only property that can be positively identified as a residence of Lewis' family. Finding an exact location for the Lewis family's residence in Caergwrle has proved more difficult. Census records from the time when they would have lived there don't contain house names or numbers. But there's a clue: Richard Lewis' house in Belfast was called 'Tŷ Isa', meaning 'Lower House', presumably a reference to an ancestral home. There's a Tŷ Issa farm about a mile and a half west of Caergwrle. It's the only property in the Caergwrle area with the right name. And it looks old enough to have been around in the late eighteenth century. Ironically, the next neighbouring property on the same hillside lane is a Christian centre called: 'Fairhaven Faith Home. Latter

Rain Mission International.' But I could not get further confirmation of the Lewis connection, and it looks as if the question of whether Tŷ Issa is really the family's place of origin will have to remain a matter not of proof, but of faith.

However, my researches did produce one other connection: Joan Lewis Murphy, a cousin of C.S. Lewis himself, and someone who knew him well, as her father and Lewis were brought up together. She too has researched the author's Welsh roots, and has visited Caergwrle. She tells me that the parish's fifteenth century church, in the neighbouring village of Hope, would have been the family's place of worship before Joseph Lewis joined the Methodists. So any pilgrim tracing the roots of C.S. Lewis will at least have something in the Caergwrle area at which to point a camera. Not Cair Paravel exactly, but a Caer all the same.

There's a Caer at Llay as well. Llay is a former mining village just north of Wrexham. Its main distinction was having, at one time, the deepest mineshaft in Britain; it went down three thousand feet. Llay's main legacy of that period is its impressive Miners' Welfare Institute. Built in 1929, Grade II listed, and recently renovated, it's a one-time fortress of working-class solidarity.

But there's another fortress in Llay too. Much older, and less well-known. It's the Caer Alyn hill fort, which stands on a promontory in a sharp bend in the river Alyn, between the villages of Bradley, Gwersyllt, Gresford and Llay.

It's possible this site was occupied as early as three thousand years ago, in the Bronze Age. It was certainly occupied in the Iron Age, over two thousand years ago. The Caer Alyn Archaeological and Heritage Trust has been gradually exploring the site for the last four years. Already, they've found layer after layer of human settlement, going right through the Roman period, to the Anglo Saxon period, the Dark Age, the Middle Ages and right up to the Industrial Revolution. It's a big site, one hundred and twenty acres, and the project team have plans to reconstruct some of the Iron Age wooden buildings *in situ*. As well as showing how their ancestors used to live, they hope to study the houses' thermal properties. Iron Age houses were cool in the summer and warm in winter, and the project hopes to find out how. As an extractive industry, this digging up of the past might not employ as many people as coal. But it could be a whole lot better for the planet.

BRYMBO STEEL

Brymbo and Steel. For more than two hundred years the two words were inseparable. Ever since John 'Iron Mad' Wilkinson had moved to the area from Cumbria in 1761 to take over the Bersham ironworks and, in 1792, had bought Brymbo Hall and started an expanded operation there. Industrial iron production was the cutting edge technology of its day, and John was an edgier character than most. He was willing to exploit to the full his profitable connections with the age's pioneers, like his brother-in-law Joseph Priestley, the discoverer of oxygen, and James Watt, who invented the steam engine, but he was just as willing to pursue vicious vendettas, such as that with his brother William, whom he shopped to James Watt and his company for making Watt-style steam engines without paying the premium to the inventor.

Legends attached themselves to Wilkinson like iron filings to a magnet. He'd been born in a market cart. He'd discovered coal tar. And coal gas. He'd built the iron bridge in Shropshire. He'd founded the Wilkinson's Sword company. None of them were true. But it was a measure of his real innovations and achievements that people could believe that these accreted stories *were* true. He was in the same league as Watt and Telford and Brunel. Telford himself called him 'The King of the Ironmasters'. He was restless, ruthless, tireless.

In every way. In his late seventies, he sired three children by Ann Lewis, his housekeeper at Brymbo Hall. The chief clerk at Bersham, Gilbert Gilpin, recalled a visit by Wilkinson in 1804 when he was seventy-six.

> He has lately been over at B. Rowley's for a few days, together with his girl. She, poor creature, while there had nearly died of indigestion from having gorged herself with eating salmon. Old Shylock and her withdrew from the table; and having laid on the bed together for a few hours, she returned perfectly recovered... Like Franklin and other great men, J.W. has written his epitaph, and I have been promised a copy of it. I have not heard its substance and am at a loss to devise what he can say in favour of himself. He reads it to all who visit him. In short, the epitaph is now the order of the day! Perhaps by making

his own epitaph he conceives he shall avoid a part of the calumny which he would be subject to were he to leave it to the world to make for him.[7]

He certainly tried. This is what he wanted:

Delivered from persecution of malice and envy, here rests John Wilkinson, ironmaster, in certain hope of a better estate and Heavenly Mansion, as promulgated by Jesus Christ, in whose gospel he was a firm believer. His life was spent in action for the benefit of man and he trusts in some degree to the glory of God, as his different works that remain in various parts of the kingdom are testimonials of unceasing labour.

This is what he got, his executors having edited it down once the great man was finally safely buried in a giant iron coffin of his own design back on his family estate in Cumbria:

John Wilkinson, Ironmaster, who died 14th July 1808, aged 80 years. His different works, in various parts of the kingdom, are lasting testimony of his unceasing labours. His life was spent in action for the benefit of man, and, as he presumed humbly to hope, to the glory of God.

He had to be buried four times. Once temporarily when his wooden coffin was found to be too big for the iron casing, and a new iron one had to be made; once, temporarily again, when the hole was found to be too small and another one had to be blasted; once – it was presumed finally – with the right coffin and right hole; and then once more, twenty years later, when the estate was sold and he was moved to a final, final resting place.

In Brymbo, his legacy lived on, as the ironworks, later a steelworks, went from strength to strength, through changing owners, nationalisation and privatisation, employing three thousand people at its height and sustaining not just the village of Brymbo itself, with its collection of steep, chapel-ended terraces in a tangled complex of hills and valleys, but also the surrounding communities as well. My mother worked there for a while, as secretary to the manager; my grandmother too, as a cook. When there were layoffs, or a strike, the whole area felt the effect. In October 1931, when the steelworks closed during the Depression, unemployment among insured men in Brymbo was 81.5 per cent, making it the highest in Wales, even outstripping the south Wales Valleys which are more commonly associated with the deprivation of the period.[8] When it was thriving – which was most of the time, as the plant had invested in some of the newest technology in the industry – the rumble of the rolling mills could be heard all night, and the sky above the village would glow red in the evening when the furnaces were opened and the molten slag tipped out onto the bank.

And then, in 1990, it ended. The works had been bought in 1986 by United Engineering Steels in Sheffield. The government wanted capacity in the steel industry reduced; the company wanted Brymbo's full order book to feed business to its Sheffield plant. So Brymbo was closed, almost overnight, or so it felt. Workers gathered round the furnaces for the last tap of steel, a bugler played the last post, the lights were switched off and the doors were closed on two centuries of history. The furnaces and rolling mill were sold to China, at enough of a bargain for it to be worth while transporting them across the globe. The local paper carried a full-page photograph of the furnace being taken by low-loader on its way from north east Wales to the Far East. 'The Chinese Takeaway,' the headline read.

Sixteen years on, I visited the site with Peter Appleton, who worked at the plant as a metallurgist for forty years, having started straight from school. Only a few of the buildings are still standing: one of the original blast furnaces, a scheduled ancient monument; and some of the sheds and workshops. Painted signs on the brick walls are guides to rituals not yet forgotten but never to be practised here again: '28-inch Mill Blades'; 'New Mill Blades'; 'Scrap Blades'; 'Buckled Blades.' You still need to wear a hard hat and high-visibility jacket to get onto the site; it feels a bit like an act of polite homage to an old faith; like donning a skullcap to visit a Jewish cemetery. But there's a reason for it. This is still an industrial site. The land where the main block of the works once stood is being redeveloped as housing. Five hundred units. Jason Parry, the site manager, shows us the plans: two-bedroom starter homes; six-bedroom executive properties; three-storey town houses; apartment blocks. There will be a new school, light industry, a call centre, child-care facilities, a cyber cafe. The Brymbo link road is being extended; There will be access to Liverpool and Manchester.

It's a huge site. Five hundred acres. Cleared of its complex of industrial buildings, it seems surprising that the cramped confines of the hills around Brymbo could have provided such an expanse of flat acreage. But it's there, ready for the latest industrialist, George 'House Mad'[9] Wimpey, to make his killing. It's a hot summer day; JCBs and bulldozers are levelling the surface. Dust devils dance where the furnaces once poured white-hot steel.

The redevelopment work has yielded one unexpected treasure. A fossil forest. Most coal measures contain fossils, of course, but this was different. They found a collection of more than twenty giant club mosses, still in their original growing positions, and surrounded by smaller horsetail plants; all of them turned into columns and veins of coloured minerals. A vegetable Pompeii. Three hundred million years ago, this was an equatorial carboniferous forest. The horsetails were the dinosaurs of the plant world. Their modern descendants are a metre high; these originals are tree-sized monsters.

Peter is part of a group trying to make sure the site is preserved. They want a geodesic dome built above it to protect the fossils from the elements. It will be the most accessible record of a carboniferous forest in the UK and part of a heritage centre preserving what's left of the ironworks too. They've produced brochures: 'Welcome to the Fossil Dome.' While the application grinds its way through the grants process, fossils stolen from the site have been appearing for sale on eBay.

We make our way back through the abandoned buildings. Girders and hooks hang from the ceiling; the floors are tangled junk and oily pools. In one of the old workshops we find the wooden patterns which were used for the metal casting. This was fine, detailed work. Most of the patterns are still on their shelves, but in the middle of the dusty floor is one by itself; a wooden plate with the metal letters resting on it, forming the words 'St Tydfil's Sunday School'. There's only one St Tydfil's around here: in my home village of Coedpoeth. The Sunday School was a metal building we called the Mission Room. I used to go to youth club there. But it was demolished a good twenty years ago, and was more than one hundred years old then, having been built in 1875. A careless knock from a foot would have turned this century-old foundry task into meaningless scrap-iron Scrabble. But it's there as though laid out especially for me to see on my one-and-only visit. Jung coined the word 'synchronicity' for this kind of thing. I take a photograph to remind myself I hadn't imagined it. We leave it in its place, and close the door.

On the bank above the workshop, Peter shows me where a colony of Great Crested Newts has been preserved. They're a European rarity. There's a special newt fence to stop them escaping. Further along there's a rarity of another kind: the 'Wonder Pit'. This former mine was so called because, unlike the troublesome coal seams of other parts of the area, where mineshafts had to duck and dive to find the elusive deposits, this one seam had no fault, allowing it to be worked like something out of a textbook, making it remarkable enough to earn it the name of a 'wonder'.

A little further down, there's the old steelworks railway line with a collection of the old equipment on it; strangely-shaped wagons and containers. It looks like a science-fiction wagon-train to me, but Peter knows each component by name: 'That's the clam shell bucket. The steel-making ladle. The crucible wagon. The crop wagon. And that's the slag pan.'

He's saddened by the closure, and by the state of the works as they are now: the skills being forgotten, the terminology becoming obsolete. We make our way down towards the site entrance to hand back our hard hats and fluorescent waistcoats. I take a glance back at the train of crucibles. They're colossal. Giant bowls of rusting, riveted iron. Looking back on them among the undergrowth that's taking over the site, they look like the Easter Island heads.

I hope Peter and his group get the heritage centre they want. All communities need some kind of mirror in which to view themselves, and, whatever its current condition may be and whatever its future as a dormitory village may hold, Brymbo has plenty to commemorate. For one thing, it was the birthplace of a prime minister.

Thomas Price, the son of a stone mason, was born in Brymbo, on 19 January 1852, and brought up in Liverpool. His was a poor family, and he started work aged ten. In 1883, he emigrated to Australia for the good of his health. The move certainly did him good – seven years after his arrival, and after becoming a union activist, he was elected to parliament, then Labour Party leadership, and finally, in 1905, to the premiership of the entire country. When he died in 1909, his fellow parliamentarians, initially sceptical because of his fiery oratory, mourned him as one of Australia's finest politicians.

He came back to Britain in triumph in 1908, and made the pilgrimage to his home village. There's a photograph of him on that visit, top-hatted, frock-coated, in the book *The Golden Age of Brymbo Steam*, by two of the village's other noteable sons, Geoff and Hugh Charles.

Geoff Charles, was born in 1909, lived at the Old Vicarage in Brymbo, and was educated at the village's Council School. He was one of the most important Welsh photojournalists of the twentieth century. In a forty-year career, he witnessed some major news events: he reported the Gresford disaster, and was the only photographer at the Le Mans racing track in 1955 at the point when a car crashed into the crowd, killing more than eighty people. Charles' photographs were flashed around the world. In Wales, his long association with *Y Cymro*, the Welsh-language weekly, saw him chronicle some of the huge social changes of the period. His photograph of the hillfarmer poet Carneddog, forced by old age to leave his home and pictured looking out for the last time at the bare expanse of hills, is an icon of a vanishing way of life. Charles' meticulous record of the destruction of the village of Capel Celyn near Bala in the 1960s to make way for a reservoir for Liverpool, is still haunting today, forty years after that notorious eviction which did so much to create modern Welsh nationalism.

There were other photographers working in Wales during the period, of course, but none were as painstaking as Charles when it came to preserving and cataloguing photographs. After he retired in 1975, he donated no fewer than 120,000 negatives to the National Library of Wales at Aberystwyth, and spent the years until his death in 2002 helping the staff catalogue them. They have now been digitised for posterity, and are available online.[11] For rural Wales, they're a record of a time, not so far distant, when people still milked cows by hand, worked the fields with animals, and when farm labourers still slept in haylofts. As for the industrial Wales from which Geoff Charles himself came, they're a record of a time when entire communities based their livelihoods on iron and coal.

Industry comes, attracted by fast profit, cheap labour and easily-won mineral wealth. And industry goes when the minerals are exhausted, or the profits fall, or when labour is cheaper elsewhere. But when it goes it leaves behind something more enduring than the slag heaps and the industrial relics which are the by-products of the short-lived alchemy of mineral, capital and enterprise. It leaves the people, and a sense of community which long outlives the industries which brought these places into being.

BRYMBO LAD

One who feels that sense of community more than most is Alan Owens. He was brought up in Brymbo in the sixties and seventies, the youngest of six. And when, after a spell as a British Army tank driver, he made his home in the United States in 1988, the *hiraeth* just wouldn't leave him alone. From Colorado Springs, he maintained the most comprehensive website about Brymbo imaginable. He called himself, and his site, 'Brymbo Lad'. He compiled memoirs, photographs, scanned-in newspaper pages, reminiscences, lists and links. Chapels, railways, schools, steelworks, shops, maps and pubs: a Welsh virtual village assembled on a computer, six thousand feet above sea level in the southern Rocky Mountains, and ten thousand miles away from Wales.

This doesn't strike me as at all strange. I know as well as anyone the lifelong spell which an upbringing in such a place can cast. Although I haven't lived in Coedpoeth for a quarter of a century, the eighteen years I spent there have formed me in a way more profound than any subsequent period of residence elsewhere, however long, could possibly do. Every month or so, I go back there in my dreams, sometimes exploring familiar paths, sometimes new ones, and often discovering ones which don't in reality exist but which should do. The dreams are always positive, the discoveries – new buildings, new views, new people – always congenial. It's a place of perpetual renewal; my subconscious mind seeming to find in the unpromising materials of a former mining village an endless supply of metaphors for security, belonging and hope.

When I began researching *Real Wrexham*, I'd planned to interview Alan by e-mail. But when the time came to start the section on Brymbo, I found he'd moved back permanently, and I was able to ask him to take me round the village in person.

He told me that, despite his experiences in the army, in New York and in Colorado, and despite a successful career in computing – including organising the launch of Microsoft's

XBox 360 game console at the Hard Rock Café in Las Vegas – nothing could compare with the 'tranquillity' he'd found in Brymbo. His upbringing there had been happy, with little TV-watching and a great deal of exploring the surrounding countryside. Now, back to stay, he's exploring the area in earnest, with the zeal of the returner and the professionalism of a data analyst (his day job), discovering abandoned workings, hidden tunnels and forgotten corners of his home patch.

"Every weekend we're not working, we pick a place on the map and go there and learn about it," he said. "I get my wellies on and go down the bank to look for something new."

Or something old. Brymbo is honeycombed with hundreds of old mine workings, capped shafts, tunnels and levels. And there's ample evidence of even earlier occupation. In 1958, workmen digging a trench near Number 79, Cheshire View, came across a stone cist burial chamber. Inside was a skeleton. Examination showed this to be the body of a man aged about thirty-five dating from the Bronze Age, around 1600 BC. Buried with him were an earthenware beaker and a stone knife, indications, it's thought, of belief in an afterlife. Removed from his hillside burial place, he's now on display in Wrexham Museum, together with an accurate reconstruction of what he would have looked like. What he was called, of course, is a mystery, so he's known simply as Brymbo Man.

Three and a half thousand years after Brymbo Man's time, I'm spending the Saturday afternoon with Brymbo Lad. We have some set objectives. I want to find the site of Plas Mostyn Mawr, which *The Lost Houses of Wales* tells me is a "once singular Renaissance house of *c*. 1650".[12] It was built, and named, for Archdeacon William Mostyn, but from its earliest days was always in danger of collapse due to being built on bad foundations on a slope. I was intrigued that such an important house was located so close to my home village, and that I'd not known about it, so I wanted to see if any signs of it still remained.

But this no-man's land between Brymbo and Coedpoeth contains many distractions for the history hunter. To get to Plas Mostyn Mawr, we parked near what's known as 'The Bottle', the remains of an old chimney from John Wilkinson's smelting works, and close to Penrhos engine house, an old winding building dating from the nineteenth century, and now a Cadw-maintained historic site. Close by too is a more recent, but still fascinating, relic of a more modern period, but one that now seems as remote as the Bronze Age or the

Industrial Revolution. It's the abandoned Royal Observer Corps' underground post, set up here in 1960 during the Cold War.

This is one of 1563 such posts built throughout Britain during the period. The idea was that the staff at these stations would watch for enemy planes and, in the event of a nuclear attack, would monitor the location of any nearby blast and the subsequent fallout. They'd do this with what passed for the cutting-edge technology of the day: the Ground Zero Indicator (a pinhole camera with photographic plates) and the Bomb Power Indicator, (a contraption using air pressure, bellows and a dial). Communication with the outside world was with landline telephones, cables, rockets and flares.

The posts were all closed in 1991, when the Soviet threat ended. But many of them still exist – as they were usually built on elevated sites, many of them have been snapped up by mobile phone operators. Brymbo's survives, largely unchanged. Externally, it looks like a grassy mound, with stubby, louvred ventilation shafts, hatches and with radio antenna masts painted a military green emerging from it. It looks like a cross between an Iron Age tumulus and a *Doctor Who* set from the 1970s. Inside, at a depth of a couple of metres, and accessed via a vertical laddered shaft, the concrete bunker itself is a time-capsule, complete with chair, worktop, wallcharts, and kettle. On the wall, a notice signed by the last Observers on duty says 'Goodbye'.[13] Thinking of the circumstances which led to the post being established, I'm glad that's the only 'goodbye' the place ever had to witness.

Opposite is the old abandoned redbrick chapel called Saron. Built as a Welsh Baptist Sunday school in 1899 as an offshoot from a chapel in Brymbo itself, it's now an empty shell, used for a while as a chicken shed, and now unsuitable even for that kind of flock. Judging by the number of hypodermics and candles we found inside, it has found a congregation of a different kind.

We crossed the fields to Plas Mostyn Mawr, which is indicated promisingly on Ordnance Survey maps with the Gothic script used for historic sites. When we get there, however, we found that Plas Mostyn Mawr is a modern farm and riding school, with a redbrick early twentieth century house in place of the old one. The older house had, we learn, survived nearby until the 1950s, but had then been demolished.

We walk on, across the hill towards Coedpoeth. I now want to explore a mystery of my own, triggered by my reading of Cledwyn Fychan's absorbing account of the wolf in Wales, mentioned earlier in the Gresford section. The book shows how wolves were a major part of the ecosystem, and also of folklore, for thousands of years before they were finally destroyed in the late medieval period due to the demands of noblemen whose favourite leisure pursuit of deer-hunting demanded that all rival predators be killed.

The wolves may have been hunted to extinction, but they left their mark in hundreds of place names across Wales. Interestingly, of all Welsh counties, Denbighshire (the historic county, which included Wrexham, rather than the modern unitary authority) has the most placenames derived from lupine associations – no fewer than thirty-six separate places which somehow or other refer to the *blaidd*, the wolf. One of these, I find, is 'Bryn Blaidd', the wolf's hill, which is in the Hafod, the valley of the river Gwenfro between Brymbo and Coedpoeth. This is a place which I knew well as a child. I can recall going there to pick flowering nettles for my grandmother to make nettle beer. And I recall her telling me of the weird occurrence she experienced here when she was young. She had been crossing these fields to visit her boyfriend in Tanyfron, and was walking about fifty yards behind a woman in a white dress who was going in the same direction. As my grandmother crossed the bridge over the river, the woman in front of her vanished completely in the middle of the open field. My grandmother, who seemed not to know the meaning of the word 'fear', said she would always have loved to meet a ghost: her vanishing fellow-traveller was the closest she ever got.

As I thought I knew this place so intimately, I wanted to see it again now I knew it was connected with a time, at least five centuries ago, when the most feared creatures in the British Isles once lived there. Using Fychan's map reference (SJ 290 517), we finally found the hill, which slopes down alongside a small brook feeding into the Gwenfro. We walked along the river bed. It's studded with lumps of coal carried from the hillside by the water. I picked one up, a shining black cube of latent energy, and put it in my pocket for the sake of a connection with my mining forefathers. As I did so, I heard Alan whisper; "Look!"

In front of us, only twenty yards away on the path, was a fox, motionless, watching us. As I straightened up, it jumped away over the river and we watched it climbing through the ferns and bracken of the opposite bank. It was much bigger than the few foxes I'd seen before, as furtive red flashes in car headlights. I had never seen a fox while out walking. As I watched it make its way up the slope, I was glad our journey to the 'hill of the wolf' had brought about a meeting with the wolf's closest living British relative in the wild.

We walked back up the old tramway which used to link the Hafod to Fron Colliery, and then cut across Offa's Dyke, which is still a marked ridge running along the side of the hill towards Brymbo. Alan tells me of the further plans he has for investigations of Brymbo's hidden history. He wants to explore the Black Lane Tunnel which ran in a straight line from Brymbo to the Wheatsheaf pub in Gwersyllt. It was decommissioned in the 1870s, and the engine used during the demolition was abandoned there, as the logistics of the demolition work meant it couldn't be brought out. I wish I could go with him. A steam engine entombed in a silent hillside for a century and more. It's the stuff of which dreams are made.

notes

1. Another miner died three days later, when an explosion blew one of the caps off the sealed shaft.
2. Senghennydd, in 1913, with 439 deaths, was the worst.
3. Cymdeithas Lyfrau Ceredigion, 2006, p162.
4. *Love in a Box* by Emma Carswell, (Paternoster, 2001).
5. Franklin Graham has also been criticised as being anti-Islam, and pro-American foreign policy.
6. See the website of Alston Jones McCaslin V, & Silas Dobbs McCaslin, whose mother corresponded with Lewis and who have conducted exhaustive research into his roots: home.comcast.net/~smccaslin2/AncestryofC.S.Lewis.html
7. N.J.Clarke, '"As others see us": Contemporary opinion of John Wilkinson and his achievements', *Wilkinson Journal* No.12 1984
8. Ferndale, at 73.9%, was runner-up. Information from the *Encyclopaedia of Wales* (Academi, 2007).
9. Only kidding.
10. Gwasg Carreg Gwalch, 1997, p90.
11. www.llgc.org.uk/drych/drych_s022.htm
12. Thomas Lloyd, *The Lost Houses of Wales*, (*Save Britain's Heritage*),1989, p31.
13. The shafts themselves are now locked. Information from the Subterranea Britannica website: www.subbrit.org.uk/rsg/roc/index2.shtml

WEST

COEDPOETH

Five generations. On each side. That's how far back my roots go in
Coedpoeth, a long hill of houses between Minera Mountain and the
Maelor plain. I was born here, in the house my father built. A bare
hundred yards away is the house where my mother was born; half a
mile further, the cottage where my grandmother was born, and,
closer still, the house where *her* mother was born. The net on the
paternal side was just as tight. The whole village was a matrix of
memories, collective and individual, the skein of kinship threading
through the houses like the footpaths which carved steep, private
shortcuts between the public, contour-hugging roads.

For most people, Coedpoeth is just a long street you have to drive
through on the A525 road from Wrexham to Ruthin. The road climbs
through Offa's Dyke at Adwy'r Clawdd, passes a string of old grey-
stone cottages and brick terraces interspersed with laagers of new
commuter homes, then narrows briefly at the hillcrest into a loose
clutch of shops, pubs and chapels, before finally widening out past
some front-gardened detached houses and heading off over the
moors to the west. There's nothing to detain you, unless you need
petrol, a paper or – at a push – a pint.

But to me, growing up, this wasn't some one-horse waystation. It
was a world. Self-contained, bounded neatly by the Clywedog on the
west, the Gwenfro on the east, and with Offa's Dyke still fulfilling its
thousand-year role as a border along the hillside sloping down
towards the lowlands of Wrexham. Even as a small child, the place
fascinated me. Once, one of my primary school teachers, speaking to
my parents in the village high street, looked down at me benignly and
said: "Of course, Grahame likes history, doesn't he?" I was pleased to
be the object of approval – teachers were village aristocracy in those
days – but I felt that honesty compelled some qualification. "Well," I
said, after a moment's hesitation, "only *local* history".

Which was true. I couldn't have cared less for the kings and queens
of the school lessons, or for the castles and palaces of the great. The
houses and terraces of the ordinary, however, absorbed and intrigued
me. I loved the way the seasons of human settlement could be deduced
and decoded from the terse messages chiselled into the hard local stone:
the inscriptions of the few houses whose builders had thought to mark
them with date plaques; the foundation stones of the seventeen places of
worship (I counted) within the village boundaries; the epitaphs in the
graveyards; the names on the war memorial (I counted them too).

I loved the placenames, particularly if they weren't recorded on any map and lived only in mouths and memories: Pentwyn; The Shade; the Hafod; Barn Hill, and my favourite, Pantywyll, 'the Dark Hollow', so called because the trees cast such a deep shadow; profound enough to inspire the imagination of whatever Welsh Washington Irving had first named it.

I loved the stories: the bridge in the Nant where a miller's horse and cart supposedly plunged over to their doom; the reputed hidden tunnel which ran to the lead mines, its entrance always eluding my searches; the moonstone in the cemetery which gave off an unearthly light when the moon was full. If there wasn't a story to fit some shady corner, then I'd borrow one from the armfuls of books I devoured from the village's small Carnegie library or the mobile book bus which came to our school. Greek legends, Roman gods, Egyptian tombs, Victorian spooks. It was all the same to me. A Coedpoeth Harold Carter, I searched for Egyptian remains in the promising yellow clay soil in the Adwy. A bespectacled Theseus, I hunted the minotaur in the labyrinth of high-walled back lanes down the Nant. The village was all the more engrossing for being haunted, even if the stories were imagined.

There were real stories which were bizarre enough, though. Like the time when the village was the scene of a gun-battle. It happened in November 1908. Drunken local youths at a travelling fair tried to cheat in a game to win a copper kettle by climbing a greasy pole. A fight broke out with the showmen, became a mass brawl, and the showmen had to use Winchester rifles from the shooting gallery to defend themselves. The police arrived to find fifteen people with gunshot wounds and buildings pockmarked with bullet-holes. The rifles were confiscated, and the thousand-strong crowd was dispersed. But once the police had gone, the crowd reassembled and torched the fair. In a later court case, the showmen were charged. They were acquitted, but it was the last time a travelling fair ever came to Coedpoeth.[1]

Then there was the case of John Evans, trapped underground when the Pentre Fron colliery was flooded on 27 September 1819, killing two of his fellow workers. Rescuers got the bodies of the two victims out, but couldn't find John Evans. They assumed he was gone for good. But his wife, Elizabeth, insisted they recover his body. They got his shroud and coffin ready, inscribed it with his name and age – twenty-six – and dug away.

A full thirteen days later, and three hundred feet down, they thought they heard a faint voice. They had. It was John Evans, still alive, "and fairly well too" he told them as they shouted down to him.

He'd survived by carving out a space in the roof of the gallery as the floodwater rose. He'd eaten candles and drunk water dripping from the roof. The correspondent of a newspaper called, appropriately, *Y Goleuad* (The Light), interviewed him shortly after he was rescued, and reported he believed he could have lived another week.[2] He kept the coffin and shroud in his bedroom as a souvenir. The other miners made a collection for him so he'd never have to work underground again. And the mine owners commissioned an oil painting of him, now in the Museum of Welsh Life in St Fagan's, Cardiff.[3] He lived another half century, dying in 1865 at the age of seventy-five,[4] and finally getting to use the coffin he had kept.

The mining industry created this settlement. The village's name itself means 'hot wood', a reference to charcoal-burning for the lead-mining and smelting industry. Coal was being dug here in the seventeenth century. Growing up, I found it eerie to think that the hill on which Coedpoeth was built was hollow; caverned and shafted with sealed-off mineworkings, whose entrances you could still find at places like Jockey Mines or Hafod. The daylight world concealed within it a realm of twisting, dark interior pathways, like ancestral vaults, as mysterious as any Cretan labyrinth or Egyptian tomb. It was like a collective subconscious, a dark counterpart to the stone-walled map of streets and alleys which I now know have formed my mind's lifelong neural pathways.

I went to school first at Penygelli Infants in the village, then the Juniors on the opposite side of the road, and then, when I was about eight, moved to Ysgol Bryn Tabor, the newly-founded Welsh-medium primary. These were the early, pioneering days of Welsh-language education, and the school, occupying part of the village's old secondary school at Tabor Hill, had an improvised air. The headteacher, Dewi Humphreys, taught three school years simultaneously in one classroom: one row learning, for instance, English, the next Geography, the next Welsh, and all chipping in to one another's lessons according to an unwritten rule – you could answer questions for classes older than yours, but not those for younger ones. For a bookworm like me, it was a dream come true.

There was something perpetually unorthodox about the place. Its very occupation of the site felt provisional, giving the whole arrangement an informal, unofficial feeling;[5] age boundaries were blurred by the mixing of the school years; cultural boundaries were blurred too. The very location seemed to emphasise the dual perspective which is the birthright of anyone born in a border area. Our classroom ran lengthways along the top of the hill ridge. From the set of windows to the west was the dark brown bulk of Minera Mountain, the western-most buttress of the Berwyns, beyond which was a wilder, welsher Wales than ours. From the set of windows to the east, the hill dropped away towards the English plain which stretched away boundlessly to the horizon. To the right, the *Mabinogion*, to the left, Man United. Turn your head one way, the dark interior; turn it the other, the bright distance. In those few years before we were bussed to high school in town, we were held in a brief, timeless stasis, on a hilltop, between two worlds.

I never knew from where Tabor Hill got its name. True, it's customary for Welsh chapels to take their names from Biblical mountains: Tabor, Hermon, Nebo, Carmel, and so on. But there was no chapel here. Perhaps it was long-demolished. Whatever, the resonance of the name remained, and when I was in Israel in 2006, I made a special trip to the original Mount Tabor to indulge a kind of displaced *hiraeth*.

Tabor is a huge smooth dome rising above the Jezreel Valley, just as the rounded hill of Coedpoeth rises above the Wrexham plain. To my eyes anyway. I went there with my friend Lydia Aisenberg, a Welsh Jewish woman from the south Wales Valleys, for forty years an Israeli citizen and a tireless worker for understanding between Jews and Arabs. The road to the summit of Tabor snakes steeply up to a church marking the reputed site of the Transfiguration, when Jesus' divine nature was revealed to his closest disciples. Looking down from the balcony, the Valley is spread out below. At the foot of the hill runs the Via Maris, the Way of the Sea, where the road from the Mediterranean has carried traders and conquerors deep inland into Asia. A few miles away is Ramat David airbase, named not after King David but the Welshman David Lloyd George, the philosemitic British Prime Minister who did so much to establish the Jewish state. Close by too is Megiddo, the Biblical Armageddon, where Lloyd George's chosen general, Allenby, scored the victory in 1917 which wrested Palestine from Turkish control, making it possible for Lloyd George to keep his promises to the Zionists to create a 'Jewish National Home.' On the hillside opposite are the villages of the Arab people whose ancestors paid the price of the Welshman's promise.

Material enough for historical reflection. But all I could think about was how similar it looked to the view from Coedpoeth: the rounded hill; the plain below. Had a Welshman come here on pilgrimage, perhaps and then named the hill in his homeland for its resemblance to this sacred spot? It's not impossible. Plenty of Welsh people had been to the Holy Land: three thousand came on the Third Crusade in the

twelfth century, and pilgrims visited periodically ever since. In the mid-nineteenth century; some even considered founding a colony in the Jezreel Valley itself, before they eventually decided on Patagonia. I looked out over a landscape which had been fought over by empires for millennia, and all I could think of was whether there was a connection with my home village. When it comes to imposing distant values on alien territory, there's nothing more imperialistic than parochialism.

Even having seen the Biblical Tabor, it's the Welsh Bryn Tabor which seems to me the original. The place figured largely in my childhood. Not only was the short street the site of my school, but it was also where my two grandmothers lived; near neighbours, and close friends. My paternal grandmother, Myfanwy Davies, kept the shop at One High Street, which had a unique combination of businesses: collecting and distributing dry-cleaning, and selling sweets from rows of glass jars. She and my grandfather, the builder Jack Davies, lived there in a house which seemed to me to have an endless series of corridors and back kitchens. My maternal grandmother, Dora Jones, lived in a tiny cottage about thirty yards away. It was demolished about thirty years ago, when she was given a replacement modern bungalow. All that remains of the cottage now is a patch of whitewash on the wall of the neighbouring property, which had formed one side of my grandmother's back yard. I'd painted this, as a child; the top of the square, now shoulder-height, was as high as I could reach then. As an adult, whenever I passed the wall, I got in the habit of touching the paint. I never really knew why. Then, one day, when I touched it in passing for what must have been the fiftieth time, I suddenly knew.

Whitewash

When I was maybe seven or eight years old,
I undertook to do a job for Nain
and paint the small backyard which used to hold
the bins, the coal shed and the washing line.
Although Nain's house has long been cleared away,
the grimy stones on next door's wall still show
the square of whitewash once as clean as day,
my handiwork from three decades ago.
And every time I walk up Tabor Hill,
I have to touch the patch of tarnished paint
to get a speck of proof that I am still
connected to a time that had no taint;
because for me there's nothing now at all
as pure as childhood's whitewash on the wall.

I gave that to my grandmother as a Christmas present, and a few
months later, read it, in Welsh and English, at her funeral.

METHODISTS, MARTYRS
AND MIKE THE DEMOLITION MAN

That funeral was held in St Tydfil's church, a late nineteenth century
barn where I myself was christened. Why this place of worship in
north east Wales should be one of only three in Wales dedicated to this
saint from the Valleys of the south, I don't know. But I know it has a
grim resonance with the fate of one of the other children of this
church. St Tydfil was a martyr, killed for her faith by pagan Saxons in
480. And, 1500 years later, this church produced a twentieth century
martyr: Winifred Davies, brought up and christened in St Tydfil's, and
murdered in 1967 in the Belgian Congo, where she was working as a
missionary nurse. She had refused to leave her patients when they
were abducted by rebels, and she paid the price with her life. Outside
St Tydfil's, a cross commemorates her death.

A few years ago, I was co-opted into the ominously-named SLAC,
the Standing Liturgical Advisory Committee (they had wisely
decided against calling it an Advisory *Group*) of the Church in Wales.
It met in monasteries and priories to debate things like whether
hearts should be 'exalted' in the mass or simply 'lifted up'. And other

matters crucial to modern life. On one occasion, we were proof-reading the new lectionary, the almanac which shows which scripture readings should be assigned to which day, and which saint should be allocated some of the prime real estate of the ecclesiastical calendar. Fame Academy, but for Saints. The Ugandan Martyrs were in. They died for their faith when Christianity was first introduced to that country. Also in the roll of honour was the Ugandan archbishop killed for standing up to Idi Amin. Then someone suggested including some other priests killed in Uganda later on. Sorry, no, the questioner was told. Not strictly martyrs. Priests, yes. Murdered, yes. But they had been simply caught up in communal violence; they didn't die *because* of their faith. So, they'd have to stay out. I was so mesmerised by these dispassionate discussions, that I didn't think about Winnie Davies until after the meeting was over. Damn it, I thought. No – sorry – blow it. She was a missionary, she was martyred, and whatever the entry rules said, she was from my home village. She had to go in. I ordered a copy of her biography, *The Captivity and Triumph of Winnie Davies*, and checked the facts. Yes, she was certainly a saint in my book. I wrote a belated application to get her recognised.

Too belated. The lectionary had just gone to press, and wouldn't be revised for a decade. Outside her village, Winnie Davies will be unremembered in her own country. Not that she would have been bothered for a moment, of course.

I think one of the reasons why the story of Winnie Davies is less well-known than it might be is because she didn't have a strong interest-group to commemorate her after her death. Although an Anglican by birth, she hadn't gone to Africa under the auspices of the Anglican church, but with a non-denominational mission. The Anglican church, slow-moving, but long-lasting and with a millennia-long memory, would have commemorated her more widely if it had felt a stronger sense of involvement with her work. But when a transient missionary group disbands, its collective memory, and its capacity for memorialising, scatters with it. Denominations have their uses after all.

And thanks to Methodism, Coedpoeth had plenty of denominations. Historically, Wales' Methodism is a different flavour to England's. It happened because Methodism's main founder, John Wesley, disagreed with his follower John Whitefield over the issue of predestination – whether the soul was predetermined to salvation or damnation. Wesley believed a person could change their eternal destiny by choice. Whitefield, following the teaching of John Calvin of Geneva, didn't. They went their separate ways, and Whitefield made a particular missionary effort in Wales. His somewhat fatalistic brand of belief went down well here, chapels styling themselves Calvinistic Methodist springing up the length and breadth of the land, quickly becoming synonymous with Methodism itself, as far as much of Wales was concerned. So when Wesley's followers wanted to establish their cause in Wales they had to distinguish themselves with the specific name 'Wesleyan Methodists', a distinction unnecessary in England, where theirs was the default form of Methodism, and where it was Calvinism that was the minority sport. The Wesleyans had a lot of ground to make up in Wales, where Calvinism had taken such deep root, and on the whole, they found pretty slim pickings, a bit like trying to sell Pepsi into a market already long dominated by Coca Cola. As much as they might be urged to come alive with Wesley, the people of Wales were pretty largely convinced that it was Calvin who was the real thing.

One of the places where the Wesleyans did have some success, though, was Coedpoeth, where Rehoboth chapel, a massive building with two stone pinnacles either side of its steep gable, was one of their national showpieces. Starting in 1840, the Wesleyans built three successive chapels on the site, each bigger than the last. When work began on the final structure in 1864, two thousand people attended simultaneous services in the village to mark the occasion. Coedpoeth's entire population today is only around three thousand. In 1864, the final building, an eight hundred and fifty-seater, had one hundred and forty members and three hundred children in the Sunday school. One of my ancestors, Tom Carrington, was organist there for fifty years: pillar of the

community, founder of the local bilingual newspaper, *Cloch Maelor*,[7] and author of a rather melancholy hymn-tune called 'Y Ddôl' which is still in the back catalogue of many a nonconformist denomination.

The tune outlived the chapel, which was closed by 1999. And in 2007 the building was demolished and the site cleared for the inevitable housing development. When I visited in late January, the demolition team were in the final stages of their work; only the porch was left. They were trying to bring it down intact to preserve the wooden framework of the doorway, a couple of thousand pounds' worth of antique wood. The workers were trying to remove an iron pinnacle at the apex of the gatepost. I asked them if I could have it. Might be able to have it made into an artwork. Sorry, they say. Already taken. Going to be incorporated into the new buildings on the site; the inscribed foundation stones too.

My preservatory instincts were assuaged for a moment. Then I wondered about the wood. In the past I've worked with the Cardiff-based sculptor Nigel Talbot, who specialises in making artworks out of salvaged timber; he shapes it, scorches it, insets it with ceramics, bolts in cast-iron cantos of poetry, inlays it with local legends, stamps it with metal stanzas, makes it a memorial, a chiselled celebration of place. He has work on display at Erddig. He teaches at NEWI. Perhaps he could make something out of Rehoboth's remains. After all, where better than a village called Coedpoeth to make an artwork out of burnt wood? I need to speak to the boss of the demolition team, Mike Davies. He's talking to a casual caller, who's pulled over his 4x4 to ask how to buy the chapel masonry. Mike is businesslike; tells him how good the stone is. "There's no shit here. It's all good stuff." He can take his pick. Won't get a better price. The caller looks satisfied, takes a phone number, drives on.

Mike's face was deeply tanned; he had gold teeth, a gold eyebrow stud, and a hooped gold earring. We spoke through the fence of the site, as his workers in the background struggled to remove the iron pinnacle from the porch before darkness fell. Work fast, while it is called the day, for the night cometh wherein no man can work. Not even demolition men. The long-departed chapel deacon over whose grave we were standing would have understood the words. I was glad he couldn't hear the other words the men were using as the pinnacle stubbornly refused to budge.

I liked Mike. Even though I'd come with curiosity rather than hard cash, he didn't begrudge me the time, even in the costly failing light of the late January afternoon.

"Should never have happened," he said, indicating the demolition. "But if I hadn't done it, Grahame, somebody else would have. This was good for another two hundred years. Could have made flats."

It could, and should. Villages like Coedpoeth have few enough distinctive architectural features, and the row of chapels on the ridge were our own serrated skyline. Not Manhattan, maybe, but ours. People might no longer want the piety, but as far as the streetscape is concerned, we could have used the variety. Soon, the village will be just one more mound of bedroom-village roofs, with no aspirational outlines against the sky.

"Do you know how much this cost to build?" Mike asks me. He's seen the original documents. I shake my head. "It cost them twelve pounds to buy the land, and two grand for the whole building. I asked a builder the other day how much he'd charge just to put up a porch like that one there," he pointed to the lonely arch which looked by now like a small nonconformist Valle Crucis, "He told me it'd be thirty-five thousand pounds. And that's without the woodwork. That doorway there will fetch a good couple of grand."

The pews have gone, intact, to a chapel in America. The two stone pinnacles which stood either side of the gable have gone for garden gateposts. What about the other timber? I ask him, mentioning my sculpture idea. He looks pained. "God, if you'd been here a few days ago, you could have had what you liked. But it's gone for fragging."

Joists, beams, roof timbers, floorboards. Fragmented, reconstituted, extruded and coming soon to a DIY store near you as kitchen tops, toilet seats, and bedroom tables. The framework of a faith experiencing Hereafter in Homebase.

The pinnacle was down now, and the men had started on the lead flashing. It hit the pavement a slab at a time. Lay where it fell.

Mike and his team are the undertakers of the architectural world, and they have the professional patience of their trade; practised, but not insincere. Time may be money, but they don't mind spending it with me, or with the old man who comes by, flat-capped, clutching a picture of the chapel he attended as a child. They stop work, gather round, listen, nod, look at the empty space where he's pointing out some vanished feature, listen some more.

Through the fence I can see a few gravestones still standing. Behind them, the two JCBs carry the demolition company's slogan: 'Clearing the Path for Business'. When planning permission was requested for this redevelopment, people were asked if they had relatives buried there whom they'd want to be moved. Only a handful replied, and their relatives were duly exhumed for reburial elsewhere. The remaining hundred or so are staying put, and their last resting place will be concreted over for the eight new apartments and their car park. I look more closely at the gravestones. One has a heart-rending Welsh *englyn* to a child who died in infancy and whose 'blush was laid in the earth'. The wind is blowing clouds of dust from the site. Some of it gets in my eye. I leave the workers talking to the old man, and move on. Demolition is dusty work, even if you're only a spectator. I needed a drink. But not just because of the dust.

LLANGOLLEN[9]

I give my brother, Mark, a call, and that night we drive over to Llangollen, the picturesque Dee Valley resort town in the Berwyn mountains. A pint in the Sun Inn, then a meal at Gales in Bridge Street. Gales is an eighteenth-century building, and, since 1977, is the area's best wine bar. I came here with my family when the place was still something of a novelty. It was my goodbye meal before I went away to college. I was eighteen years old. At some point during the evening I visited the bathroom. Behind the door they had a copy of the prose poem 'Desiderata':[10] "Go placidly amid the noise and the haste...". It's on many walls, of course, and in many memories. But until then, I'd never come across it: "You are a child of the universe, / no less than the trees and the stars; / you have a right to be here. / And whether or not it is clear to you, / no doubt the universe is unfolding as it should." No doubt. I had plenty of doubts, actually, of course, especially at the point of leaving home, and the poem's would-be soothing words seemed to emphasise rather than allay them. A quarter-century later, 'Desiderata's' counsels of perfection seem as unattainable as ever. I wonder if the poem's still there behind the bathroom door, ready to provide uplift among the air fresheners? I visit the bathroom, but, of course, 'Desiderata' is long gone. Back at the bistro table, we order another couple of glasses of wine – after all, as the poem says: "strive to be happy."

Being happy is something Llangollen does rather well. It has good eateries – culinary champion Dai Davies, ('Dai Chef') has his restaurant here too – and the town is a serious drinking destination for Wrexham people looking for a night on the (small) town. It's also where another Dai Davies, the former Wrexham and Wales goalkeeper turned natural health practitioner, has his healing centre. Perhaps it's the sense of protection conferred by the surrounding hills that makes the place seem like a refuge.[11] In the eighteenth century, Llangollen was the place to which the Anglo-Irish aristocrats, Lady Eleanor Butler and the Honourable Miss Sarah Ponsonby, eloped to escape unwanted marriages. They lived together in

Llangollen in the half-timbered manor house, Plas Newydd,[12] in what their contemporaries delicately called 'more than sisterly affection'. They were cultured types, much visited by the literati of the day, including William Wordsworth, who called on them and wrote a sonnet, 'To Lady Eleanor Butler and the Honourable Miss Ponsonby, Composed in the grounds of Plas-Newydd, Llangollen', which is notable not so much for its literary merit, but for his celebration of the fact that the two were 'sisters in love', and for the fact that Wordsworth managed to work a bit of Welsh into the English iambic pentameter, fair play to him: "Glyn Cafaillgaroch, in the Cambrian tongue, / In ours the Vale of Friendship..."

He was right about the nature of the place. Llangollen has made healing, happiness and friendship into an art form – literally. Since 1947, the town's annual International Musical Eisteddfod has drawn thousands of people from across the world to the Dee Valley every July for a week of music and dance competitions, and concerts. Llangollen introduced the world to Luciano Pavarotti (1955) and Placido Domingo (1968), and has played host to the likes of Dame Kiri te Kanawa, Lesley Garrett, Bryn Terfel, James Galway and Montserrat Caballe. It was commemorated by Dylan Thomas in 1953, when he described the visit of the Oberkirchen Children's Choir, of 'Happy Wanderer' fame, as 'angels in pigtails'. It was a tribute to the healing magic of Llangollen that in less than a decade after the bitter conflict of the war, the children of the former enemy could be welcomed as 'angels'.[13]

It's a tradition that the visiting choirs and dance troupes are billeted with families in local villages, as a means of keeping their costs down.

Coedpoeth played host to a different choir every year, most notably a Zulu choir from Soweto who visited during the apartheid era, and whose extended stay left a lasting impression on a community whose only previous experience of Zulus was watching Stanley Baker and Richard ("I'm Jones from Bwlchgwyn") Davies[14] fight to the death with them in the 1964 film of the same name. The dance troupe's farewell performance, complete with bare-breasted women, created a sensation which those who witnessed it – this was a north Wales mining village in the 1970s, remember – will take with them to their graves.

As children we'd be given the day off school to visit Llangollen, and I'd take an autograph book to get the signatures of anyone in national costume. The Eisteddfod seemed a natural part of the year's activities, rolling round as regularly as Christmas or Easter. So when, in 2003, I was offered a commission by the Prince of Wales, the Eisteddfod's patron, to write a poem to celebrate the festival, it was natural to agree.

But I knew little about the Eisteddfod's origins. So I went to the library and typed 'Llangollen International Eisteddfod' into its computer search. Two books came back – one the glossy official history, and the other a small, amateurishly-produced, typewritten booklet. As I gave this a quick scan, prior, I expected, to setting it aside, I was intrigued to see it was actually written by the Eisteddfod's founder, a man called Harold Tudor. I was even more intrigued to find he was from Coedpoeth. I was surprised too, as, despite my lifelong interest in local history, I'd never heard of him.

The book told how, during the last months of the Second World War, Harold Tudor had gone out one Sunday morning into the countryside near Coedpoeth. As he rested against a tree, he heard a local

farm boy singing a Welsh hymn as he delivered milk from farm to farm. In that moment, Harold Tudor had a vision of using music to unite the warring nations. He would create an Eisteddfod of music and dance. And it wouldn't just be for Welsh people; it would be for everyone.

He took the idea to the National Eisteddfod of Wales, suggesting they have an international day. But the all-

Welsh-language festival said no thanks; it had enough on its hands rebuilding itself after the war. He then looked for a town to sponsor his project, eventually deciding on Llangollen, not least because of its outstandingly beautiful location. He gathered a committee, who enthusiastically took up the idea, and developed it. In 1947, the first festival was held, was a success, and the rest is history. The Eisteddfod went on from strength to strength.

But it went on without Harold Tudor. He and the committee fell out in late 1947 over his suggestion that the festival move to another town. He withdrew, and not too many years later was having to pay like anyone else to get in to the festival he himself had founded. This hand-typed volume I had found in the library was his attempt, late in life, to record his achievement.

I was touched by this, and resolved that I'd at least give Harold Tudor his due in the poem sequence. So I put together a poem about the vision that had come to him that morning in Gwern-y-Gaseg Road. After completing it, I mentioned to my father what I'd done.

"I knew Harold Tudor," he told me. "He was our patron."

"I see."

"I know Lawrence Roberts too."

"Who's Lawrence Roberts?"

"The boy. The boy who was singing. I was in school with him. Do you want his number?"

The next night, I was sitting in Smelt Farm, Coedpoeth, talking to the man whose song had unwittingly given birth to a dream. Only twice in the sixty years since 1945 had anyone interviewed him about it, and initially, he was a bit reticent whether he could remember the details. But he could. He could even remember the name of the horse he was leading – Flower – and the name of the hymn he was singing; it was '*I bob un sy'n ffyddlon*'. As we spoke, it turned out Lawrence Roberts knew not only my father but my grandfather well, and that my grandfather had built the house in which we were talking. That meeting made a poem.

Catalyst

He's rarely told this story, so it's slow,
our conversation by the farmhouse fire.
The flames inside the blackened grate grow higher,
the shelves of horsebrass decorations glow.
It's years since anyone came here to inquire
if it was he, in wartime Denbighshire –
it must be nearly sixty years ago –
whose '*I bob un sy'n ffyddlon*', served to show
how music could be stronger than barbed wire.
But yes, in early nineteen forty five,
he was the one whose tune was overheard
one Sunday as he led his horse along,
not knowing that he'd brought a dream alive
how hatred could be healed without a word
and all the world be reconciled in song.

I completed the sequence in a few days. Then, with a couple of weeks still to go until the premiere at the Eisteddfod, my mind went back to the question of commemorating Harold Tudor, but with something more permanent than a poetry reading. A slate plaque, I thought. Just the thing. I checked with Coedpoeth Community Council whether, if I donated a plaque, permission would be forthcoming to place it on the village library. Delighted, they said.

As it happened, I was in Blaenau Ffestiniog that week on business, and, as it's the slate capital of Wales, I called to see a slate engraver, gave him the wording, and ordered the plaque. I went back to Cardiff feeling a warm glow of altruism.

The warm glow became a cold shiver that night. The phone rang. My father. He'd just had a phone call, he said, but he'd told the caller that it was to me he should be speaking. My father gave me the caller's number, in the English Midlands, and urged me to ring it straightaway.

I did, and was answered by Peter Tudor, a man who told me he'd been in school with my father, although he'd lived for decades now in Staffordshire. He launched straight into telling me that he had been looking through his own father's personal effects and had come across his birth certificate. "I don't know if you know," he said. "But my father founded the Llangollen Eisteddfod. And the poor old chap's rather been forgotten". By this time I did know that fact, but I said nothing as he continued.

Finding the certificate had spurred Peter Tudor to visit his father's birthplace with a view to commemorating him. So he'd driven to Coedpoeth and had visited both the house where his father had been born and the house where he was living when he'd had the vision of the Eisteddfod. Then, walking through the village, he'd come across a poster for the recently-formed local history society, and thought that, if nothing else, he'd join that. Getting home to Staffordshire he called the society's chairman. My father.

"Well, I'm going to surprise you now," I said.

"Oh?"

"I've just ordered a plaque to your father. And I've arranged for it to be put up on Coedpoeth library."

There was a pause.

"I don't believe it!"

"I don't believe it either," I said.

A couple of weeks later, Mr Tudor and his wife attended the Eisteddfod for the premiere of the poems, as the personal guests of the Prince of Wales.

"If only Dad could have been here," said Mr Tudor.

"Hey," I said, thinking of the extraordinary, benign coincidence leading up to that evening. "I think he is."

Compatriot

Every year they came, the travelling tribes:
Australians so tall our Celt-sized beds
could not contain their southern hemisphere frames;
Soviets who, delivered to the decadent Dee valley,
mysteriously lacked the roubles to fly home;
Zulus who, to thank our village for its welcome,
danced bare-breasted outside the parish hall,
so that even the statue on the war memorial,
its eyes downcast in municipal mourning,
couldn't help but stare.
Every year we went,
since I was boot-high to a Cossack,
glad to swap a day at school
for this rainbow rendezvous in the Berwyn hills,
to collect the autographs of Scots or Magyars,
and have our pictures taken with white-kimonoed girls,

never thinking for a moment it was strange
that every summer the nations should gather
beneath World's End,
in freedom, fellowship, and fancy dress.

Every year, still, I go,
as much for the memory as the moment.
And even though the journey now
is many miles from Llan,
many years from then,
somehow I need to see it all the more,
this one-week vision of a world made right.
And if you've watched the things you've cherished die,
or seen what hate can do, or bitterness,
violence or unforgiveness, you'll know why.

HORSESHOE PASS

The main A542 road climbs northward out of Llangollen towards
Llandegla and Ruthin, passing the chain bridge and the restored steam
railway to the left, and the site of the Eisteddfod on the right, and then
heading into the hills for a journey which is a lesson in natural beauty
and how humans have left their mark upon it.

Valle Crucis Abbey is one of the most striking historic monuments
in Wales. It got its name, which means the 'Valley of the Cross', from
the fact that a ninth-century high cross – now a stump of carved stone
thanks to Oliver Cromwell's Taliban-like distaste for carved symbols –
stands nearby. Known as the Pillar of Eliseg, it was put up to commemorate Elisedd ap Gwylog by his great-grandson, the king of
Powys, Cyngen ap Cadell. The name 'Eliseg', although carved on the
pillar, is believed to be a long-lived typo by the stone carver, who
might be forgiven this slip when it's considered that his carving task
was one of the longest of the period. It's certainly one of the longest
Latin inscriptions to survive from pre-Viking Wales.[16] It gives Elisedd's
genealogy together with some of his achievements, which included
defeating the English "with his sword and with fire", a description
which always reminds me of Sellar and Yeatman's classic spoof history
of Britain, *1066 And All That*,[17] in which all victories have to be
achieved 'by fire and sword' in order to count as real history.

Eliseg, or Elisedd, was already history when Madog ap Gruffudd

Maelor built Valle Crucis in 1201, as a daughter house for Strata Marcella abbey near Welshpool. It was a foundation of the Cistercians, the order favoured by the native Welsh princes, and which, in return, supported Welsh freedom in a battle against the English which by that time had been going on for something like seven hundred years. Valle Crucis, a tall vaulted building on the valley floor, was the last

major Cistercian foundation in Wales. It lived through the final defeat of the native Welsh dynasties in 1282, and, just over a hundred years later, the successful revolt of Owain Glyndŵr, who took his name from nearby Glyndyfrdwy. A legend tells that after Glyndŵr was finally defeated and was a fugitive, the abbot of Valle Crucis was walking in the grounds one morning when he saw a shadowy figure approaching from the mist. The figure greeted him: "You have risen early, my Lord Abbot." The abbot, recognising Owain, replied: "No. It is you who have risen early, and by a hundred years." The comment is meant to indicate a prophecy of the rise, a century later, of Henry Tudor, a Welshman who actually gained the crown of England. Owain disappeared into the mists again; whether he was a ghost or the real prince, the abbot never knew.

A day of heavy mist is probably the best kind on which to visit Valle Crucis now. Guidebooks and websites often have their pictures of the abbey buildings very tightly cropped. For good reason; it's to exclude the real view which greets the visitor: the huge Abbey Farm static caravan park, occupying a site twice the size of the abbey's, and with its ranks of giant shoebox rectangles marching right up to the gaunt outline of the ruined nave. Early English meets Lego.

The imposing remains of the Abbey Church on the outskirts of Llangollen comprise nave with aisles, choir and two transepts, each with its aisle and chapels and a short presbytery.
(National Library of Wales guide to religious architecture of Wales)[18]

Atlas Everglade 32' x 10', 2 bedrooms, 2005 model, site life of 13 years price £12,950.

... electric hook ups, shower and toilet facilities and a number of seasonal pitches available.

(Abbey Farm Caravan Park advertisement)[19]

The park is immaculate, the static caravans – 'Ozokozi', 'Spion Kop', 'Rubberneck Bend' and their neighbours – are spotless. However, the recent winter storms have upended and trashed one touring caravan, which stands upside-down next to the wall by the abbey nave.

Valle Crucis Abbey was finally dissolved in 1536 under Henry the Eighth's purge of monastic institutions, and was one of the first religious houses in Wales to actually be emptied and destroyed. Viewed from the hillside road, the caravan park's two double semi-circles of outsized white oblongs look like a pair of colossal dentures about to crunch the abbey ruins like a walnut, and finish the work of dissolution for ever.

A mile or so further on, and the gradient on the A542 steepens as it climbs one of Wales' most spectacular roads, the Horseshoe Pass, an old turnpike road built in 1811 and known in Welsh as 'Bwlch yr Oernant', 'Pass of the Cold Stream'. Cold it can be too. It often closes in wintry weather, a necessary precaution, because, with a drop of around fifteen hundred feet into the valley below, any danger here can be lethal. In 1998, a three-day search for a missing grandfather and his thirteenth-month-old grandson ended here when the car was found crashed at the bottom of the pass, the grandfather dead, but the boy, miraculously, unharmed and alive.

On the hillside at the centre of the horseshoe is a concrete pillbox,

built around 1940, and located to command a view up both sides of the pass in the event of the Nazis ever reaching the Dee Valley. From inside the strongpoint, you realise that its defenders would have gained the security of the concrete walls only at the cost of having a severely limited field of vision and an impossibly, ultimately suicidally, static position.

Further up again is the entrance to one of this area's

many slate quarries. Slate quarrying is mainly associated with north west Wales, but there were extensive and profitable slate deposits in Denbighshire too, and they were worked at least from the seventeenth century. One of them is still in business: Berwyn Slate's Clogau quarry, 1360 feet above sea level.[20]

The slate industry has left the Horseshoe Pass with one of its most popular unofficial attractions: the so-called Blue Lagoon, an abandoned quarry pool popular with swimmers and divers. Its real name is Moel y Faen, 'The Bare Hill of the Stone', but, like a placename in some Native American language, it's been supplanted by later arrivals wanting something easier to pronounce and more familiar to their own cultural reference points – in this case a name taken from a film about two young children shipwrecked on a Pacific island. There have been three versions of *The Blue Lagoon*: a silent one in 1923; a classic black-and-white version with Jean Simmons and Welshman Donald Houston in 1949, and a saucy 1980 version with that year's teenage temptress, Brooke Shields, featuring full-frontal nudity. There's a possibility of full-frontal nudity at Llangollen's 'Blue Lagoon' too, as the Welsh Wild Swimming Association, which aims 'to preserve the historic right to river swim and to introduce a new generation to this most ecological and healthy of pastimes' notes it as being suitable for skinny-dipping.[21] But don't expect to see Brooke Shields there.

A combination of the richness of the scenery and poverty of the imagination seems to have give this whole area a nomenclature suited to a Western novel or a child's treasure map. There's the 'Horseshoe Pass'. Or the 'Panorama Walk', which skirts the slopes of the mountains to the west. And the 'Blue Lagoon.' It's not even original: quarry pools the length and breadth of the UK are called that. And just across the way is the other major recreational feature of the area: 'The Ponderosa Cafe'. The Ponderosa was the name of the ranch where the hugely-popular 1950s, 60s and 70s TV cowboy series, *Bonanza*, was filmed. The Llangollen Ponderosa is hugely popular too. It's an extensive complex of low buildings with a restaurant, cafe and gift shop, a

magnet for tourists and coach parties, and particularly with motorcyclists, who use it as a high-level rendezvous.[22]

On the Sunday lunchtime I visited, there were scores of bikers there from all over north Wales and north west England. Their machines filled the car park: Yamaha, Suzuki, Honda, the odd rumbling Norton and Triumph. Inside the cafe, the radio was blasting out the Mexican-style trumpet flourish at the start of Johnny Cash's 'Ring of Fire'. The bikers were queueing obediently, trays in hand, for their bangers and beans. All the place needed was bat-wing doors.

The Ponderosa is quite a rendezvous for sheep as well. Out on the open moorland, there's nothing to stop the sheep coming down to the car park to scavenge among the picnickers. Which they do, in large numbers. On a busy summer's day, when scores of cars are parked on the moorland on either side of the cafe, the sheep are an amusement for the visitors. Outside tourist times, though, they can be a blasted nuisance for any tired walker who dares to sit down to have a bite to eat. Ponderosa sheep are a genetic mutation, fed on crisps, chocolate and sandwiches. For them, human beings hold no terrors, only opportunities. They crowd round, butting and shoving, while their fellows stream down from the hills to join in.

Looking east from the Ponderosa, the sweeping bluffs of the Eglwyseg rocks stretch in a spectacular, swelling series of curving limestone cliffs. There's nothing like them in Wales. Further east, and hidden by the hills, is a place with another of those names that sound as if they've been made up for a cheap novel: World's End. Perhaps, for all the fact that its earth is trampled by trippers and scarred by scrambling bikes, there's something about the sheer treeless openness of this mountain, and its huge expanse of sky, that makes people think in ultimate terms. It's seen more than one suicide, as people have taken themselves to this highest point to end their lives, as if trying to get as close as possible to heaven before ending their time on earth. One of the most tragic cases was in March 2003, when a farm labourer from Cheshire killed himself and his four young sons by filling their car with carbon monoxide gas. The roadsign next to the fateful layby is now a makeshift shrine, with scores of teddies and soft toys left there by well-wishers. Denbighshire council have agreed with the family to replace the untidy toy tributes with a memorial bench. But for the time being, these orphaned playthings keep a perpetual vigil on the windswept roadside, a damp mound of mourning.

It was here too that one of Wales' most famous novelists met his death. George Alexander Graber – pen-name Alexander Cordell – was born in 1914, the child of British parents, in what was then Ceylon. Although he later claimed Rhondda roots for his mother, his upbringing was that of a typical officer-class product of Britain's waning colonial empire, and gave little suggestion of his later career as a writer of rumbunctious and pungent novels of south Wales industrial life. His love affair with Wales began when he moved to Abergavenny, and developed an interest in the history of the south Wales Valleys. In 1959, this resulted in his first successful novel, *Rape of the Fair Country*, the story of the spirited Mortymer family. It became a worldwide bestseller, translated into at least seventeen languages.

Critics may have found its style – in which the characters' English speech is heavily flavoured with syntax and sayings translated from Welsh – to be derivative of Richard Llewellyn's 1939 classic, *How Green Was My Valley*, and it certainly lacked the cathartic personal mythologising of Llewellyn's novel. But all the same, there's more real history in Cordell's novels than in Llewellyn's, and there's no doubt that Cordell's work had a vigorous life of its own. Although 'vigorous' hardly does justice to Cordell's world of two-fisted brawlers ("His hair was black with curls and his face square and strong. He stooped, moving easily from the waist, and I sensed the power in him,") and tempestuous beauties ("Pretty enough to take the breath, this one, with her long slim legs and her breast white and high-curved above the petticoats"), where the people of every Valley seem to have swallowed verbal viagra ("'*Dammo di!*' said my mother. 'What a life it is! Charters and

Unions, torchlight processions, Benefit clubs and secret meetings. Down to Abergavenny with me, I think and join the Quakers or wear sackcloth and ashes, and to hell with the damned old cooking.").

Cordell could keep that up for a whole book. In fact, he kept it up for another six long historical novels about Wales, as well as numerous novels on other subjects too. And once the convention of his style is accepted, the Welsh novels have an undoubted power to make the closely-researched history come alive. In the late 1980s, as a means of acquainting myself with the history of the Valleys, where I was living at the time, I read all seven in sequence. *Rape of the Fair Country* (1959); *The Hosts of Rebecca* (1960); *Song of the Earth* (1969); *The Fire People* (1972); *This Sweet and Bitter Earth*, (1977); *Land of My Fathers* (1983), and *This Proud and Savage Land* (1987). Duw! Great crash course in Valleys history, it was. Played hell with my speech patterns, it did, mind.

During his writing career, Cordell lived in various parts of Wales, but he spent his final years at Rhosddu in Wrexham. Here, my father and he became friendly; they shared the same military background, as former Royal Engineers, and the same profession, as quantity surveyors.

Cordell's second wife died at the Maelor Hospital in 1995 at the age of eighty. The end for Cordell himself came two years later, in July, 1997. Two local farmers, out mending fences, found his body on the mountainside near the Horseshoe Pass. The circumstances were as extraordinary as any which the imagination of a novelist with a taste for the melodramatic could have devised. Cordell's body was found in a kneeling posture, as though in prayer, with his head on the floor; a bottle of brandy was set on the ground in front of him, with pictures of his first wife, Rosina, and his second, Donnie, propped against it. He had with him seven Temazepam anti-depressant tablets. Back home at Rhosddu, he'd left a suicide note.

But whatever his intention may have been, it seems that death came to him without assistance from spirits or tablets. At the inquest in November that year, a pathologist's report showed Cordell had no alcohol in his blood and only the slightest trace of Temazepam. But he did have such a bad heart condition he could have died at any time. It appeared that after setting out the brandy and the photographs, he had actually suffered a natural heart attack, possibly brought on by the climb up the mountainside. The coroner concluded that, whatever may have been in Cordell's mind, he had died of natural causes.[23] As an end to a life of storytelling, the manner of his death was even stranger than fiction.

Follow the road out toward Llandegla and turn back to Wrexham across the moorland, and you find yourself approaching Bwlchgwyn, which is, its sign tells you, the 'Highest Village in Wales'. It's easy to believe, as you round the corner and see the Cheshire plain and the flat sprawl of Merseyside set out like an aerial photograph far below. But is it true? There are at least three other villages in Wales which claim to be the highest. The notorious Penrhys housing estate, built in 1968 on top of the ridge between the Rhondda Fawr and Rhondda Fach valleys in south Wales, 1400 feet above sea level, makes the claim. So does Garn-yr-Erw in Torfaen which is 1279 feet above sea level. And so does Llangurig in Powys, near the source of the river Wye. It's 1000 feet above sea level. Bwlchgwyn is 1090 feet, or 333 metres. Which means that if it's to be sure of first place, it needs to find another 310 feet somewhere. Maybe there's room for the kind of enterprise shown by the fictional villagers in the Hugh Grant film, *The Englishman Who Went Up A Hill And Came Down A Mountain*, where they add a huge cairn to the top of their mountain to make sure the mapmakers don't downgrade it to a mere hill. Still, Bwlchgwyn is definitely the highest village in north Wales. And that '1400 feet' figure for Penrhys sounds suspiciously round. Who's to say those south Walians can be trusted with their measurements anyway?

WORLD'S END

There's another route to Wrexham from Llangollen too, a short cut heading roughly eastwards across the moors. This way passes the base of Castell Dinas Brân, the ruins of a thirteenth century native Welsh castle on a steep, isolated hill overlooking the valley. This is 'Carbonek', the home of the Fisher King, and the place where Sir Galahad finally finds the Holy Grail – or so Arthurian legend has it. Legend has a lot of things about Castell Dinas Brân. Stories congregate around it like crows: it was named after Bendigeidfran, Brân the

Blessed, the giant hero of the *Mabinogion* myths; there's a golden ox buried deep within it; it's an abode of the fairies; there's a golden harp hidden there; evil spirits will attack whoever spends the night on its summit. It's been more successful as a myth-magnet than it ever was as a stronghold: it's possible that as a traditional castle, it was only occupied for a couple of decades by the princes of Powys before being destroyed by Edward I in 1277 and never rebuilt.

That, however, didn't stop the novelist John Cowper Powys setting a substantial part of his novel *Owen Glendower* in a largely-ruined Dinas Brân at the turn of the fifteenth century. Although born in Derbyshire and raised in Dorset, Powys cherished family legends of being descended from the princes of Powys – he had the name after all – and he moved to Wales in 1934, living until 1955 at number seven, Cae Coed, Corwen, only a few miles from Llangollen.[24] Finding himself in the valley from which that other descendant of the princes of Powys, Owain Glyndŵr, took his name, he quickly identified with the Welsh freedom fighter, and in 1941 produced a mammoth work of nearly a thousand pages with his own individualistic version of Glyndŵr's mission. As is characteristic of Powys' work, the external events become ciphers for internal processes which hold deeply symbolic personal meaning for the author, if not always for his readers. The following extract gives a fair idea of his style. The italics, and the exclamation mark, are Powys':

Rhisiart stared inquisitively at these pitiful stones, for they lay in heaps in every direction, and he tried in vain to imagine how the place looked in the heyday of its glory, before the treachery of his own ancestor had left it to alien hands.

One curious effect these ruins had on him as he waited in the draughty damp-smelling darkness, along with the Lollard and the mad Friar, was to evoke such a different Dinas Brân from the one that he had imagined that it was no longer a rival to the imaginary one and no longer mingled with it or impinged upon it. All the while he had been approaching the real Dinas Brân, that other, that mystical one which he had created in his childhood, had kept blending with it, had kept rising out of it and beyond it into more fabulous, more enchanted towers. But now as he stood in the dim guard-room, listening to Mad Huw's irreverent whispers and quiveringly conscious of the dark nerve which Lowri had set twitching in his inmost being, these two Dinas Brâns *separated completely*. The imaginary one lifted itself clean out of this draughty mad-house of broken stones, of which

Lowri was the evil spirit and wherein he must meet 'burning' with 'burning' and limned itself on those flying cloud-wracks of the mind's horizon that no madness could touch and no burning blacken!

That Dinas Brân, painted with mystic pigments upon a spiritual canvas, rose up still in its immortal air, clear of all these tumults.[25]

In trying to recapture today the sense of how Dinas Brân would have been when it was inhabited, it certainly helps to have an imagination, even if not necessarily one quite as pigmented with mysticism as Powys'. Of the medieval structure, only a few ruined walls remain, with a rough arch and a shapeless window; it looks like a child's sandcastle in the last stages of dissolving. But the view is worth the tough climb, and the sight of the dark bulk of the Welsh mountains to the west, and the Dee snaking through the valley on its way to the plains of England, is enough to make even someone with a monochrome materialist imagination see what made this place appealing to princes, novelists, and the makers of myths.

On the opposite side of the valley, where the Panorama Walk skirts the edge of the limestone plateau, another myth-maker is commemorated. A mile or so along here, in the direction of Trevor, is a monument to the poet Isaac Daniel ('I.D.') Hooson, (1880-1948) from Rhosllannerchrugog. The son of a local draper, he was born, lived and died in Victoria House in Market Street, Rhos. A solicitor by profession,[26] he was also the local Official Receiver, but was known throughout Welsh-speaking Wales as the author of deceptively simple and affecting lyric poems and of a popular 1934 adaptation of Robert Browning's ballad 'The Pied Piper of Hamelin'. Hooson provided a wealth of children's poetry, a scarce commodity at the time.[27]

Hooson, a lifelong bachelor, had no children himself. But Ena Woolford, who with her brother, David Wyn, spent much of her childhood at Victoria House, where their grandmother and aunt were housekeepers, remembers him as her unofficial grandfather. She recalls that every Saturday evening in summer, he would drive up to the Panorama Walk with his lifelong friend John Johnson, a local tobacconist, and they would walk up to the ridge, and sit for hours looking out over the valley. After the poet's death, in 1952, this was the place chosen for his ashes to be scattered and for his memorial to be built.[28] Ena was asked to unveil it, overcoming her initial shyness after being reminded that this was a means of repaying Hooson for his kindness. "I had never been up there until that day," she told me. "But it's a beautiful spot. It's no wonder he loved it."

The mountain separating Llangollen from Wrexham is a plateau of silurian and ordovician shale rocks, divided roughly in half by the Eglwyseg river valley, feeding westwards into the Dee near Llangollen. To the north-west of the divide is a mountain called 'Cyrn y Brain', which means the 'horns of the crows', or possibly 'horns of the ravens', the Welsh language being somewhat imprecise when it comes to black-coloured birds. To the south-east, the plateau is known by various names, depending on the nearest community: 'Ruabon Mountain', 'Rhos Mountain', 'Minera Mountain', or 'Coedpoeth Mountain'. All things to all men. The Ordnance Survey map hedges its bets, giving 'Ruabon Mountain' and 'Minera Mountain' in two places, with 'Esclusham Mountain' on the Llangollen side. Pasted broadly across the top and referring to the beauty-spot gorge more or less in the middle of the mountain, are the words 'World's End'.

At the base of the gorge stands Plas Uchaf, an impressive timbered house, mainly Tudor, but with parts dating from the fourteenth century, and possibly built on the site of a Roman settlement. It's connected with the twelfth century legend of Owain, Prince of Powys, who, infatuated with his married cousin Nest, abducted her from Pembroke Castle, where her husband was steward. He's reputed to have taken her to his hunting lodge of Plas Uchaf, giving a new meaning to the term 'Love Nest'. In fact, although the kidnap is documented, the actual place to which Owain fled is not given.

But Plas Uchaf tends to attract legends like that. For instance, there's the one I heard as a child, that Winston Churchill and Herman Goering stayed there between the wars to shoot grouse. I never questioned the story until I heard the same claim made about another country house elsewhere in Britain. And then about another, until I realised it's one of those urban myths – or rural myths in this case – which attach themselves to any likely-looking location. The author Byron Rogers has investigated a similar phenomenon in which various hotels are claimed to have been visited by Kaiser Wilhelm prior to the outbreak of the First World War.[29] Perhaps the World's End story, bogus though it is, hints at a truth: that national elites often co-operate when it suits them, and that their allegiances can be changeable. No doubt in the nineteenth century, people were claiming something similar about Napoleon, and further back, peasants were probably saying; 'See that manor house there? Well that's where that William the Conqueror stayed with King Harold a few years before the Conquest'. Plas Uchaf does, however, have a real historic connection. One of its former occupants was Colonel John Jones, who married the sister of Oliver Cromwell. It's not quite as good as Churchill and Goering shooting grouse, but at least it's true.

MOUNTAIN ROAD

The cliffs around the gorge follow an orderly naming convention, as though christened in a batch: Craig y Forwyn (The Maiden's Crag); Craig yr Adar (The Birds' Crag); Craig y Moch (The Pigs' Crag); Craig y Cythraul (The Devil's Crag), and Craig Arthur (Arthur's Crag). From their slopes, several streams feed into the headwaters of the Eglwyseg, which is forded by the single-track road between Llangollen and Minera. From the ford, a steep first-gear climb takes you up to the empty bracken-covered plateau, 1200 feet above sea level. It's claimed you can see Blackpool Tower and even the Lake District from the heights here on a clear day. I've never seen that far myself, although Liverpool, closer by, is clearly visible, as is the Wirral peninsula, a flat rectangle of land cut out by the silver blades of the Dee and Mersey estuaries.

There's also a tradition that you can see many of the historic counties from here.[30] The number varies, but it includes Denbighshire (easy, you're *in* Denbighshire); Flintshire, (yes, only a mile or so away to the north); Cheshire and Shropshire (yes, both of them are spread out obediently right there to the east) and Lancashire (yes, it's that jumble of grey on the eastern bank of the Mersey estuary). More doubtful, but possible, are Staffordshire and Derbyshire (that lumpy outline on the eastern horizon could be the Peak District), and Westmorland and Cumberland in the Lake District. You need the eyes of faith, or a very good telescope, to see those last ones. What's not in doubt, though, is that the view eastwards is one of the most stunning in Wales, and there's no other place where the contrast between the Welsh highlands and the English plain is so stark, or where geography underlines history so emphatically. The one side open, flat, orderly, sunlit; its roads straight and broad, its horizon stretching to infinite distances and possibilities; the other side secretive, mountainous, unruly, shadowed; its paths narrow and twisting, its horizons bounded closely by the next dark hill.

The mountain, scattered with Bronze Age stone cairns, was used until recently as a grouse moor; a line of shooting butts still marches across it. Now it's common-land grazing for sheep, a footpath for walkers, a scenic drive for tourists, a place to pick whinberries, a vantage point for radio hams, and a place to dump and torch stolen cars. There are a few sheep farms on the slopes, and the stock is free to roam. Today, there's a cattle grid preventing the sheep leaving the high ground, but when I was a child, the same function was served by a gate, a hassle for drivers travelling over the mountain, but an income opportunity for an enterprising child, who could earn a useful amount in tips by opening the gate for approaching cars. The trick was not to open the gate too early, or they'd just drive through – you had to keep it closed until the car had to slow; then open it with a flourish. The drivers would then throw coins out of the window for you to pick up. Why they threw them rather than just handed them over, I can't imagine, but that's what they did, and as long as I got the cash to take home to put in my Dalek-shaped money box, I didn't much care.

The mountain carries the signs and scars of earlier enterprise too: mineral working and prospecting. The moorland is studded with the remains of old mineworkings and kilns. Midway across is a group of these, and in the middle, the concrete base of what had once been a gamekeeper's cottage, all that remains after the building was destroyed in a gale. As a teenager, this was a favourite place for me to come on my motorbike to do my A-Level revision.[31] Given the results that I got at A-Level, I might have been better off revising in a library. The peace and quiet of the hills was supposed to promote study. I suspect it promoted daydreaming.

I was distracted by other things at that age as well. Teenage love affairs, of course, (in which the mountain also played a role). But more lastingly, and more successfully, literature, and Wales, which I had discovered when I was about sixteen, with all the intensity of a first love; more intense, in fact, and more long-lasting. I read everything I could about Wales, obsessively, indiscriminately – the scholarly and the crackpot, the authoritative and the irresponsible together, not knowing or caring which was which: Thomas Parry's masterly *The Oxford Book of Welsh Verse*; Trevor Fishlock's urbane and affectionate *Talking of Wales*; Meic Stephens' conscientious and troubling *The Welsh Language Today*; Roy Clews' credulous 'history' of the Free Wales Army, *To Dream of Freedom*; Y Lolfa's book of Welsh drinking songs (although I knew of no pubs where I could join in singing them), Emyr Llewelyn's atavistic plea for a return to a simpler, welsher Wales, *Adfer a'r Fro Gymraeg*; Richard Llewellyn's *How Green*

Was My Valley, a tear-jerking vision not of how Wales was, but how it should have been, and, of course, George Borrow's *Wild Wales*.

Borrow had walked this way too. While staying in Llangollen, he took the journey over the moors, using as an excuse the desire to buy a new book on Welsh Methodism from Wrexham. "If one wants to take any particular walk it is always well to have some business, however trifling, to transact at the end of it," he said. At the beginning of his journey, at World's End – although he doesn't record it by that name – he encounters a householder at Plas Uchaf who praises him as "a person of great intelligence" for his knowledge of Welsh. Then, at the Ruabon end, he greets a local collier in Welsh, who, although he understands Borrow, insists on addressing him in English: "How's this?" he asks Borrow: 'Why you haven't a word of English? A pretty fellow you, with a long coat on your back and no English on your tongue, an't you ashamed of yourself? Why, here am I in a short coat, yet I'd have you to know that I can speak English as well as Welsh, aye and a good deal better."

The man storms off, refusing to speak to Borrow further. Borrow, however, was philosophical about the encounter, regarding it as an example of nemesis: the collier on one side of the mountain repaying him with an insult for the over-praise he'd received from the farmer on the other.

A traveller who attempted to use Welsh with strangers on the same route today would need to be equally philosophical, equally thick-skinned, but also extremely optimistic.

CLYWEDOG VALLEY

Poison, an air battle, an unsolved murder, treason, execution, an alleged massacre, and a riot, all in a few miles' walk. None of this is in the guidebook for the Clywedog Valley, which emphasises only the peace, the woodland and the relics of former industry. But it's all here if you want to look for it. The fortunes of empires have been, if not actually decided in this secluded valley between Minera Mountain and Wrexham, then certainly reflected here.

The poison to begin with. Lead poison to be exact. The local carboniferous limestone around Minera holds extensive lead deposits, and has been mined possibly since before the Romans started mining here and elsewhere in north east Wales, in the second half of the first century AD.[32] Many ingots have been found with the word

'Deceangli', the Latin name for the local Celtic tribe, which gave the area its Welsh name 'Tegeingl'. The name 'Minera' itself has been suggested as being of Roman origin. The Romans wanted lead for water pipes and for cooking and drinking vessels. It didn't rot or rust; it was cheap and plentiful, and was easy to work with. However, it was also, unknown to them, a deadly poison, and this is how Minera played an unwitting part in bringing down the Roman empire.

From the late nineteenth century, scholars have speculated whether lead poisoning contributed to the fall of Rome. The theory goes like this.[33] Roman upper classes got their water through lead pipes, which causes lead poisoning. Even more destructively, the aristocrats made extensive use of a syrup made from boiled-down grape juice as a preservative and a sweetener. The problem was, they boiled it in lead vessels, which meant that the syrup was a sweet, slow and deadly poison, as the boiling process had infused it with lethal levels of lead. As a result, the Roman upper class, the only people who could afford the luxury of the syrup, suffered chronic infertility, madness, and deadly illness. This, the theory goes, explains all those mad emperors during the empire's last years; it also explains why the patricians died too quickly and had too few healthy children to renew their ranks quickly enough to keep control of the plebeians. Scholarly opinion is divided over the significance of lead poisoning, but it's certainly true that that many Roman corpses have shown evidence of abnormally high levels of lead in their systems. *Quod Erat Demonstrandum*: Minera helped bring down the Roman empire.

A later empire suffered something of a setback in this area too. The Nazi Third Reich. The moorland overlooking Coedpoeth is an unlikely site for a battleground, but that's what it became for three nights from 31 August 1940, when a lone German bomber, returning after trying to bomb Liverpool, jettisoned its payload, setting the dry bracken of the mountain alight. From the air, the burning mountain looked like a major target had been hit, so whole flights of German bombers returned on the following two nights to bomb what they thought was a blazing city. The British were only too happy to let them believe that – better that the bombs fell on empty moorland than on a packed city. Lord Haw Haw, the Nazis' propaganda voice, even mentioned the raids as a success. In fact, the bombs were falling harmlessly on the empty hills. By the end of the raid, twenty-eight square miles of the mountain were ablaze, and many Scousers owed their lives to Minera Mountain's three-night decoy act.

The valley between the mountain and Coedpoeth is called Pantywyll, which means 'dark hollow'. It certainly has dark connotations, as it's the location of one of the Wrexham area's most notorious unsolved murders. It happened in 1945, when a young woman called Caroline Evans went down the valley from Coedpoeth to visit her mother at the City Arms pub near New Brighton. She never got there, and her body was later found strangled in a copse at Pantywyll. An RAF forage cap was found near the body, but despite this clue – or, as it may have been, this red herring – her murderer was never found. Caroline Evans is buried in the cemetery overlooking the place where she met her death. The grave looks as weathered as though it were from the nineteenth century. Caroline Evans' murderer, however, might still only be in his seventies. The police reopened the case in 2006, and, if the killer is still alive, this news might have caused a shiver down an elderly guilty spine somewhere. But at the time of writing, the mystery was no closer to being solved.

From Minera, the Wrexham road passes the little hillside village of New Brighton, with its visitor centre, restored lead mine and its little black-painted Presbyterian tin chapel called Hermon. In their day, places like this were frontier townships: stake a claim, throw up the ter-

races for the workers to live in, and a tin chapel for them to pray in, give the place a name – a deliberately ironic one in this case[34] – and start digging. If you hit paydirt and prospered, the place would grow, and the chapel be replaced by a masonry one. If not, then it would stay as a rusting reminder of what might have been.

There's another tin church half a mile away along the Wrexham Road: St Andrews,

Wern. These buildings, once common, are now becoming rare. St Andrews features on the website, Tin Tabernacles[35] which seeks to record these sanctuaries before they become scrap-iron. The tin chapels were erected as a quick and temporary religious fix for fast-developing industrial communities; but like the prefabs of the Second World War, although not built to last, they lasted.

Built to last, but demolished, is Wern chapel, a few hundred yards away. This was the home ground of William Williams of Wern, (1781-1840) one of the three most influential Welsh preachers of his age, and a charismatic crowd-puller and church-builder. The chapel he founded was demolished in 1960, leaving only the shell. The mountainside graveyard, containing Williams' memorial, is now a forgotten, bramble-choked wilderness.

Where the Wern road turns down towards Bersham is the site of Plas Cadwgan, once one of the most important medieval hall houses in Wales. Based on a former barrow and motte-and-bailey castle site, the thirteenth century house was home to Edward Jones, a prominent Welsh Catholic executed in 1568 for his part in the Babington Plot, a scheme to have Elizabeth the First replaced with her Catholic cousin, Mary Queen of Scots.

The Crown confiscated Plas Cadwgan, and it passed to the Myddleton family, and in 1855, became part of the Plas Power estate. The previous year, George Borrow had passed it on his travels, describing it as: "strange-looking... very large, ruinous, and seemingly deserted".[36] Quizzing a woman in the doorway of a nearby cottage, he found that it was used only for storage, that it had once been a bar-racks and was reputed to be haunted.

Despite its neglect, it survived a century more, into the late twentieth century, as the tallest and best-preserved medieval hall in Wales. But that couldn't stop a new owner demolishing it, "a disastrous loss made worse by the circumstances," according to Thomas Lloyd, author of *The Lost Houses of Wales*.[37] The site, immediately on Offa's Dyke, is now home to a modern ranch-style farmhouse. The outbuildings are still ancient, though, and part of the site is occupied by a huge, partly excavated Bronze Age tumulus, already fabulously old when Offa was putting up his earthwork. It's reputed that four full sets of armour and a horse's skeleton were found here in 1797. Some of the interior of Plas Cadwgan survives at the Avoncroft Museum of Historic Buildings near Bromsgrove in Worcestershire, which managed to save the timber frame, "re-erected in more grateful England", as Thomas Lloyd put it. Whether the ghost travelled to the Midlands isn't known.

NANT, RHOSBERSE, PLAS POWER

The Clywedog river crosses Offa's Dyke in a part of Coedpoeth known as the Nant, where there's a well-preserved water mill, now a visitor attraction. Running parallel to the dyke at this point, at right angles to the main road, is Rhosberse Road, bounded on the Wrexham side by the high wall of Plas Power estate.

It was in one of the cottages on this road that my own grandmother was born in 1906. Her father, William Thomas Hollywell, was a miner and union leader. She told me that when he used to walk back from the mine along the lonely road in the early hours of the morning, he would be followed by ghostly footsteps. Always too afraid to look round, he would knock at the door of the cottage to be let in, by which time his hair would be almost standing on end from fright.

As a teenager, always fascinated by ghost stories, as I still am, I decided to put this haunting to the test and walk the road at night myself. However, I was too wary of doing it in pitch darkness, so I compromised by going at twilight, and for company, I took my grandfather's dog, Cymro.

For the first few minutes, our walk was uneventful. Then, unmistakeably, from nowhere, I heard the crunch of a footstep. A pause, and then another. I looked round; there was still enough light to see, but apart from myself and Cymro, there was no-one in sight. On the one side were open fields, and on the other the high wall of the Plas Power estate. The road ran straight and clear in both directions. We walked on. Crunch. Pause. Crunch. Unmistakeable. Inexplicable.

By this time, my own hair must have been standing on end, and I was glad I had the dog with me. Crunch. Crunch. Crunch. Nothing in sight, and yet the sound was as though it was coming from the air around us. We approached a gap in the wall, and as we drew level with that space, that was when I saw it.

A cow. An ordinary black-and-white, common-or-garden Friesian. Hearing our footsteps on the other side of the wall, it had followed them, as cows do in their aimless amiable manner, plodding along silently across the field, and cropping the grass every few paces as it did so. That cropping was the crunch I'd heard.

Was this the explanation of the ghostly footsteps my great-grandfather had heard? Certainly this noise would have sounded even louder in the pitch dark. I went home convinced I'd solved the mystery. Wrexham Paraskeptics,[38] the local group who investigate strange phenomena, would have been proud of me.

But there's another mystery associated with Rhosberse Road, and one for which there's no such easy explanation. The fields on the Wrexham side of the wall were an American army camp during the Second World War. And according to several sources, they were the scene of a hushed-up incident in which soldiers were killed for going absent without leave.

Leslie Kynaston, who was a teenage boy at the time, and who lived at Rhosberse farm, immediately next door to the camp; told me what happened. We spoke in his home, the lodge to the Plas Power estate, only yards from the farm where he lived at the time of the incident.

He told me that in May 1944, his father had returned from Wrexham one afternoon in a state of shock. He told the family that as he'd approached the junction with Rhosberse Road, perhaps ten minutes walk from the farm, he'd seen a car in front of him stop and an American soldier get out. As the soldier did so, a shot rang out, killing him. He then saw other soldiers collect the body and throw it into the back of a lorry where there were bodies of other GIs already lying.

Later that day, Leslie Kynaston himself saw soldiers from the camp set up a machine gun in the entrance to the site next door to the lodge house. The gun was pointing outwards as if to prevent intruders. This had never been seen in all the time the GIs had been at the camp. He went and spoke to the soldiers, but apart from one of them telling him he was from Texas, he couldn't find out what was going on.

By that time, the family had heard that a number of GIs had gone absent without leave from the camp, and that other soldiers had been sent to round them up, and that the deserters were being shot on sight. This seemed to be confirmed later that night when some American soldiers called clandestinely at the farm.

"It was about twelve or one o'clock, and I heard some shouting," said Mr Kynaston. "There was a group of Yanks, about sixteen or seventeen of them, and they wanted to get back to camp because they were being shot. They were looking for another way in. I went downstairs, and they gave me fags, about three hundred, and I sent them down to the river where there was a roadway down through the wood. It was a moonlit night."

In the days following, rumours circulated in the village about the incidents, but American army camps during World War Two were literally a law unto themselves under the Visiting Forces Agreement, which made United States soldiers subject to their own military laws rather than those of their host country, so facts were hard to come by. Besides, a matter of weeks later, the entire camp was emptied as the

Americans went off for the D-Day invasions. The camp was then used for German and, later, Italian prisoners of war.

Sixty years on, the episode still troubled Mr Kynaston, who said he hated to think of those men's deaths being unrecorded, or, possibly, falsified.

Seeking further information, he wrote to a local newspaper, and received one piece of corr-oboration from a Mr J.C.Durkin of Southport in Lancashire, who

said that his brother James, who served in the Welch Regiment, was in the Wrexham area at the time, and reported that more than fifty soldiers had been shot over a twelve hour period. He makes reference to a similar incident in Preston, where American soldiers were indeed shot by their own side during a disturbance at camp. This was the so-called 'Mutiny at Bamber Bridge', which happened on 23 and 24 June 1943, when several black GIs were shot by other American troops after a fracas which was essentially a racial conflict between black troops and their white counterparts.

Further details of the Wrexham incident have proved elusive. But it's not so hard to believe that some killings could have happened when you recall that only twenty-four years previously, and only twenty miles distant, five Canadian soldiers were shot dead in a riot at Kinmel Park camp near Bodelwyddan on 4 March 1919. This happened after more than a thousand of the Canadian troops had rioted, frustrated at delays in returning them to Canada after the war. Four of the five are buried at the Marble Church at Bodelwyddan, along with many other Canadians who died at the camp from the influenza epidemic of that year.

So the possibility of American soldiers meeting a similar fate a generation later within the walled confines of their camp is not beyond the bounds of possibility. The figure of fifty deaths sounds exaggerated, but it's possible that, as with Kinmel Park, there could be a kernel of truth in the Plas Power story. But without the evidence of the burials, only American veterans could tell the true story, and, more than sixty years after 1944, and with Mr Kynaston himself having now died, that trail's quickly going very cold.[40]

BERSHAM

You have to be careful with these legends. The Clywedog river continues down the valley past the remains of the Plas Power park, which still contains traces of the old formal gardens, until it reaches Caeau Weir. The weir is built in a series of steps like a wide staircase. They're known locally as 'The Russian Steps' because they were built by Russian prisoners of war during the First World War. Spot the mistake? Yes, Russia was an *ally* during the First World War. And besides, records show the steps were actually built in 1911, three years before that conflict began.

A few hundred yards on, just before the village of Bersham, is a church whose claim to fame is that it is almost certainly the only private place of worship in Wales still holding regular services. It was built by the Fitzhughs, the gentry family who acquired the nearby eighteenth century Plas Power hall through marriage in 1816, and who are still prominent locally even though the hall itself was demolished after the last war. They built St Mary's Esclusham in 1875 in richly-decorated Romanesque style. The church's bell tower was added more than forty years later, in memory of Captain Godfrey Fitzhugh, killed aged forty-four in Palestine in 1917 on the first day of the Third Battle of Gaza.

The three battles of Gaza had cost thousands of Welsh lives – the Allied army had a disproportionately large Welsh contingent thanks to the desire of Prime Minister David Lloyd George to have a 'Welsh' army conquer the Holy Land. Conquer it they did, sweeping past the Turkish defences of Gaza on 31 October 1917, and capturing Jerusalem on 11 December that year, with the Wrexham-based 24th Btn. Royal Welch Fusiliers taking part in the attack.[41] Welsh troops led the march into the holy city and formed the first Christian guard at the Church of the Holy Sepulchre since the Crusades. It made a great story for the enthusiastic audience back home. 'Capture of Jerusalem… Enemy Driven Back by Welsh Troops' was the *Western*

Mail headline that day. Referring to the implications for the Zionists, a subsidiary headline recorded 'Rejoicing in Jewry'.

But there was mourning in many places too. Captain Fitzhugh, of the Royal Welch Fusiliers, (25th Montgomeryshire and Welsh Horse Yeomanry Battalion), is buried, with more than a thousand other Allied casualties, at Beersheba cemetery on the edge of the Negev desert, in a place now near a modern shopping complex and over-shadowed by high-rise flats. Captain Fitzhugh's widow Ethel had the bells installed at Bersham in his memory, and they still ring every Sunday, their musical eight-bell carillon a connection with a battle which was one of the most decisive of history and whose repercussions are still being felt around the world.

There are echoes of other world-changing conflicts immediately next-door too. Although Bersham today looks like a picture-postcard village, with its steep-gabled, diamond-paned estate cottages, it was once the equivalent of BAE Systems, a high-tech arms manufacturer whose products could decide the fate of nations.[42] It specialised in cannons. Ironworking began here in the seventeenth century, when the factory made weapons for the Royalists in the Civil War. By the eighteenth century, the works had passed to the Wilkinson family; first to Isaac Wilkinson, and then to his energetic, inventive and ruthless son John, whose career was discussed earlier in the section on Brymbo.

By the last quarter of the eighteenth century, John Wilkinson was producing the smart weapons of the day: smooth-bore cannons. He'd greatly improved the effectiveness of the heaviest military technology of the period by producing a smooth bore, preventing the weapon jamming, and making it much more accurate. The guns were used in the American Revolutionary wars, and right through into the Napoleonic period. The works were also the scene of a chaotic row between John and his brother William, when William sent a gang to destroy the works as an act of revenge, and John took the opportunity to contribute a gang of his own to the work of destruction. It's supposed that John's motives were that he saw this as a means of dissolving what had become an intolerable partnership with his brother without going to the expense of a law suit; the wrecking would let him carry off the most expensive pieces of machinery by force for profitable use elsewhere. He was a hard man to beat.

notes

1.   Glyn Davies, *Not Long Ago*, (Megan Kelly, 1984), p24.
2.   *Goleuad Gwynedd* of November 1819, Robert Edwards, *Coedpoeth As It Was* (Coedpoeth, Star Press, 1991). Available in full on the BBC Wales website:
     http://www.bbc.co.uk/wales/northeast/sites/wrexham/pages/john_evans.shtml
3.   Colin Gibbs, *Clatter of Clogs*, (Bridge Books, 1990), p63.
4.   He's buried in Adwy'r Clawdd chapel graveyard.
5.   After I left, it moved to the vacated English infants school down the hill, where it grew and thrived. The original buildings are still there, a youth centre now, still looking improvised.
6.   David Michael Davies, (Hodder & Stoughton, 1968).
7.   Emyr Evans, 'Rehoboth Coedpoeth, Dymchweliad yr Adeilad.', *Y Clawdd*, No 120, January 2007, p12, p13.
8.   Edwards *op. cit.* (Star Press, 1991), p30.
9.   Not in Wrexham borough, but formerly part of Denbighshire and Clwyd, and subject of two local referenda on transferring it to Wrexham. The first, in 1993, went firmly to Wrexham, the second, seven years later, to Denbighshire, by nine votes. A subsequent Assembly inquiry kept the town in Denbighshire.
10. Often presented as anonymous and 'discovered in a church' in 1692, but actually written by American lawyer and author Max Ehrmann, (1872-1945) and copyrighted by him in 1927.
11. Frank Serpico, the New York policeman who exposed corruption among his fellow-officers and was a target for death-threats, lived in Corwen for a while in the 1970s to 'get his head together'. Al Pacino played him in the 1973 film *Serpico*.
12. Now open to the public, and a place of pilgrimage for students of nineteenth century lesbianism.
13. The first visit of German competitors to Llangollen, a Luebeck choir, actually took place in 1949. This visit is often conflated with the later, better-known visit of the Oberkirchen 'angels'. But it had a special poignancy of its own. Eisteddfod compere Hywel D. Roberts had lost his brother Glyn fighting the Germans in 1944. Asked to introduce a choir from the country of the former enemy, he found himself saying the words: "Please welcome our friends from Germany".
14. Sadly, there's no real connection between Wrexham's Bwlchgwyn and Rorke's Drift, and the Welsh connection with the battle itself is much weaker than the film suggests.
15. Literally 'To each one who's faithful,' sung to the tune 'Rachie', by Dr Caradog Roberts (1878 – 1935), of Rhosllannerchrugog.
16. Now illegible, but recorded in 1696 by antiquarian Edward Lhuyd.
17. Methuen, 1930.
18. www.llgc.org.uk/ardd/pensaeri/arch010.htm
19. http://www.abbeyfarmcaravans.co.uk/)
20. Owned by the Bickford family of Swansea since 1991.
21. www.swimming-holes-wales.org.uk/
22. www.ponderosacafe.co.uk/index.html
23. *The Daily Telegraph*, 14 November 1997.
24. He was visited there by Simone de Beauvoir and Jean-Paul Sartre, and on a separate occasion by Henry Miller. http://knowhere.co.uk/4011_heroes.html
     http://homepage.ntlworld.com/elizabeth.ercocklly/top10non.htm
25. John Cowper Powys, *Owen Glendower*, p261.
26. His office, Hooson & Hughes, was in Egerton Street.
27. Meic Stephens, BBC Cymru'r Byd:

www.bbc.co.uk/cymru/gogleddddwyrain/enwogion/llen/pages/id_hooson.shtml

28. Inscribed 'Bardd. Eisteddfodwr. Cyfaill i Blant Cymru', recording his status as poet, supporter of the eisteddfod, and Friend to the Children of Wales.

29. *The Bank Manager and the Holy Grail: Travels to the Wilder Reaches of Wales*, (Aurum Press, 2003).

30. Not the current local authorities.

31. Once, standing here on a windless summer evening, I was mystified by a sound like an invisible train coming closer, surrounding me and then receding. Sometime after, a local gamekeeper explained it to me as the sound wave from a collapse in one of the mining levels honeycombing the mountain.

32. My own great-grandfather part-owned a small lead mine in the area.

33. Jerome O. Nriagu. 'Saturnine Gout among Roman Aristocrats' *New England Journal of Medicine*. March (1985), p660-3.

34. There are two other New Brightons close by: one small village near Mold and the other, a substantial former resort near Liverpool. The name was common as a sobriquet for new towns in the English-speaking world, although usually they were by the sea, not deep inland.

35. www.tintabernacles.com/

36. *Wild Wales*, Chapter 62.

37. *The Lost Houses of Wales* (Save Britain's Heritage, 1989), p30.

38. http://www.wrexhamparaskeptics.4t.com/home.htm

39. Mutiny at Bamber Bridge:
http://www.bbc.co.uk/ww2peopleswar/stories/85/a3677385.shtml

40. Williams *op.cit.*, (p310) notes the unit based at Plas Power was the 83rd United States Army Hospital (OC Colonel F.G. Norbury), and that it departed in June 1944. The 83rd Infantry Division was also based in the area during the period. Several memoirs by veterans of the 83rd are online, many mention training in Wales; none mention any incident at Plas Power.

41. They then spent Christmas in Bethlehem. Williams, p107.

42. There's a small heritage centre at the former Bersham school.

SOUTH

RHOSLLANNERCHRUGOG

It was the morning of my first-ever visit to New York City. With my wife and two young daughters, we'd decided that before doing anything else, we'd take one of the open-topped Big Apple tour buses to get an overview of the place. As is the way with tour buses, people get on and off at every stop. As we were heading down into Wall Street, a large group got on. One of them sat on the vacant seat next to me. I took no notice, intent on taking in the stupendous view of the skyscrapers, familiar from so many movies, but which I was now seeing with my own eyes for the first time.

One of my daughters turned round to say something to me. I replied briefly, not taking my gaze from the vertiginous vistas of office windows on every side.

But I'd replied in Welsh. My neighbour turned to me as though she'd heard a gunshot.

"*O ble 'dach chi'n dod?*" "Where do you come from?" The eternal Welsh greeting. Nothing you've achieved; nothing you've become; no place you might be, matters as much as where you've come *from*. Be it twenty years ago or sixty. Who you were is who you are. Forever.

Don't get me wrong. Belonging's great. It's good to know who you are, who your people are; to stay in touch with your roots. It was just that I didn't want my genealogy examined just *then*, when I was wanting to take in that mythical-yet-real landscape to the full. I could do roots anytime. I could only get my first glimpse of New York once. I decided to be polite but vague.

"North Wales," I replied, with a brief smile which I hoped satisfied the demands of tribal loyalty. I looked back at the buildings. So this was Wall Street. Gordon Gekko. Michael Sheen. Martin Sheen. I tried to imagine a ticker-tape parade.

My interrogator leaned closer.

"*Where* in north Wales?"

"Mm...Wrexham." Same smile. A bit briefer this time. Back to the buildings. The crash of 1929. Would people have actually have jumped from those ledges?

There was a note of real excitement in my questioner's voice now.

"*Where* in Wrexham?"

I could feel the net closing.

"Coedpoeth."

"I'm from Rhos!" Triumph. I was captured. Pinned down to within a mile of my childhood home with three well-placed questions. Faster than GPS. I'd been reeled in from my fantasy of a stateside escape back into the familiar web of Welsh kinship. Forget the gleaming skyscrapers of the Lower East Side. We were now back in North East Wales, retracing well-trodden paths through the redbrick terraces of the past. There was no hiding behind generalities now. The skyscrapers would have to wait. Proximity took priority. There were obligations to be fulfilled. I sighed inwardly, and got on with it.

"So you must know..." I named a local councillor whom I'd met on a couple of occasions.

"Of course! He's my cousin! And you must know..." She named a local schoolteacher.

"That's right. He taught me in school."

And so we went on, until, at the next stop, my neighbour, and the Rhos contingent, left *en masse*. Perhaps they'd spotted someone else from Wales.

My wife turned round to ask who had been those people I'd been talking to.

"From Rhos," I answered. She turned away again. That was all she needed to know. Although she is herself from south Wales, she knew enough about my home area by this time not to be surprised. Rhos people get everywhere.

Or they seem to at least. In Wrexham folklore, the person from Rhos is supposed to be regarded with some suspicion. Cohesive, committed to education, hard work and 'getting on', Rhos people were traditionally prominent in the civic, cultural and educational life of the Wrexham area, leading to the usual whispered accusations of clannishness and nepotism which afflict the successful members of any identifiable community. Perhaps it's something to do with the sheer size of Rhos. As villages go, it's big, with around ten thousand people if you include Johnstown, Penycae and Ponciau. On that demographic power-base rests its boast of being the biggest village in Wales. And maybe that claim itself says something about the pride for which its inhabitants are famed. Not the biggest city, no. Not the biggest town either. But by God, it's the biggest village. When you're one of hundreds of overlooked former industrial communities around the country, you take your pride where you can get it, and even though Rhos is certainly bigger than many towns, it would rather not compete in the big pool of urban centres. In the small pool of Welsh villages, however, Rhos is one big proud fish.

Too proud, some people in neighbouring communities would say. The former MP, Tom Ellis, a native of Rhos,[1] recognises this tendency:

he says people accused Rhosites of 'bumptiousness'. However, he says: "our response was to laugh at them and accuse them of envy."

They had plenty to be proud of, though, like many mining communities where hardship bred solidarity, a determination to achieve and a respect for education. Like all such communities, those characteristics are now declining like a worked-out coal seam. But you get a taste for the kind of culture places like this produced if you talk to someone like Tom Ellis. After our visit to Gresford colliery, he and I called at the sites of the Hafod and Bersham collieries, where he used to work, and which had provided the economic bedrock of Rhos and the surrounding district. He recalls that when he worked there, Welsh was overwhelmingly the main language of the workers at Hafod.

We share an interest in Welsh literature in both languages. He's an author, local historian, a friend of statesmen, of poets and painters, a collector of art, of rare first editions. In the course of a few minutes' conversation at the pit-head, interspersed with anecdotes about former mining colleagues, he's quoted Sartre; "To speak an oppressed language is a revolutionary act... it is to attack capitalism in its softest spot." And T.S. Eliot's treasured endorsement of the value of the Welsh language: "It is the instinct of every living thing to persist in its own being." And Yves Person, the Breton historian who challenged what he called '*imperialisme linguistique*'. And R.S. Thomas:

> We continue our relationship
> with the young David, flooring
> the cheque-book giant
> with one word taken,
> smooth as a pebble, out
> of the brook of our language.[2]

And Aristotle and Plato too. You don't need to know all that to run a mine, or run for Parliament. But this was the kind of big-picture thinking that those cultured mining communities fostered, in the days long before the phrase 'think globally, act locally' had been invented.

It had its lighter side too. In his absorbing biography *After the Dust Has Settled*[3] Tom Ellis tells of a friend of his father's, a committed socialist, who visited the Soviet Union in the 1960s to see the May Day parade in Red Square. When he got back, Tom Ellis asked him for his impressions of Russia. He answered with conviction.

'Tom, we have been misled about Russia, scandalously misled. I shall tell the people of Rhos.'

Other factors contribute to Rhos' separateness. For one thing, there's the question of geographical isolation. The main road bypasses it at some distance, meaning you only ever go to Rhos on purpose, never on the way to somewhere else. It had its own newspaper, the *Rhos Herald*, until the 1960s, and even today, although the Wrexham area has its own monthly Welsh-language community newspaper or '*papur*

bro' called *Y Clawdd* (The Dyke) Rhos insists on its own separate one, called *Nene*, a word peculiar to the Welsh dialect of the area: it's pronounced 'nair nair' and is a pronoun meaning 'that' or 'that thing'. Rhos dialect is distinctive, and Welsh speakers, hearing my own accent, which is similar, often think I'm from Rhos myself, not realising the great gulf represented by the mile or so distance between that village and my own. It's like being a Canadian and having people constantly mistake you for an American. You get tired of having to explain, but you have to do it. If you're a Canuck, you don't want to be a Yank. And if you're from Coedy, you most certainly don't want to be a Jacko.

A Jacko? The generic term for a native of Rhos. Apparently it dates from the late seventeenth century and early eighteenth century when Jacobites, supporters of the Stuart dynasty deposed from the thrones of England and Scotland, were expelled to Rhos from Wrexham town centre. *The Encyclopaedia of Wrexham* notes there was a 'secret' Jacobite society known as 'The Cycle of the White Rose' in existence in Wrexham from 1710, and that Jacobites attacked two Dissenters' meeting houses in the town in 1714. The 'Cycle' itself mutated into a highly-respected social club for the local gentry, and survived until the mid nineteenth century.[4] Nothing dies easily in Rhos, though, and the nickname has long outlived the cause that created it.

Another major factor in the area's distinctiveness is the strength of the Welsh language there. Even in 2001, the census showed forty-nine per cent of people in the Ponciau ward, including the northern part of Rhos, reporting one or more skill in Welsh.[5] The Pant ward in the village centre showed forty-four per cent, and neighbouring Penycae, Ruabon and Johnstown, which include parts of Rhos, showed thirty-

five, twenty-three and thirty-three per cent respectively. Impressively high figures for communities within walking distance of the English border. Only in the last decade or so did Welsh become a minority language in the area, a fact which, when combined with the village's strong choral and educational traditions, made the community a kind of musical equivalent of the mythical Outside Half Factory of south Wales.

Certainly, the reputation for ubiquity which surrounds Rhos people has something to do with the prominence of their exported human capital. The roll call of famous exports includes the composer Arwel Hughes, (1909-1988); his son, the conductor and presenter, Owain Arwel Hughes (born in Cardiff but still counted); and composers John Tudor Davies and Caradog Roberts (1878-1935). Roberts was responsible for the rousing hymn tune 'Rachie,'[6] to which the hymn '*I Bob Un Sy'n Ffyddlon*', known in English as 'Who is on the Lord's Side?', is always sung. As mentioned in the section on West, this was the tune which, when sung by Lawrence Roberts in 1945, inspired Harold Tudor to establish the International Eisteddfod. The choral tradition continues in full spate today, with two rival male choirs: Rhos Male Voice Choir and the Rhos Orpheus Male Voice Choir; a ladies choir and – to make sure all gender permutations are catered for – a mixed choir. There's even a Pensioners' Choir. In Rhos, no substantial demographic group is without a choir of its own.

Rhos has produced outstanding individual performers too, such as the tenor Geraint Dodd and the young piano virtuoso Llŷr Williams, who has won seemingly every top prize for pianists worldwide, and whose amazing ability to memorise music was first noticed by his father when he saw his son absorbed in reading a complicated score in a music shop.

'Shall we buy it?' he asked him.

'No thanks', said Llŷr. 'I've read it. There's no need.'

There wasn't either. From a single read-through he could play the whole piece from memory. It must have saved him a fortune in sheet music.

In the acting world, there's Meredith Edwards (1917-1999)[7], who began his career with Lord Howard de Walden's embryonic Welsh National Theatre at Plas Newydd in Llangollen. After the war, he moved into film and television, not allowing his former status as conscientious objector stop him taking roles as servicemen, most notably in the 1958 film, *Dunkirk*, where his character is mortally wounded, and John Mills' character is forced to abandon him, mumbling his dying words in Welsh. Edwards had to persuade the director to let him deliver the lines in his native tongue. [8]

A modern actor from Rhos, Mark Lewis Jones, also rarely seems to be out of uniform, of one kind or another. I remember Mark as a stocky, bruising member of our school rugby team. Now in his early forties, he's made a name playing stocky, bruising types in tough dramas: the homophobic squaddie brother in the iconic nineties drama series *This Life*; the anti-semitic brother of Ioan Gruffudd's character in the Oscar-nominated 1999 movie *Solomon and Gaenor*, and Tecton, 'a bull-necked captain of the elite Apollonian Guard,' in the 2004 Brad Pitt Trojan War epic, *Troy*. In the 2003 seafaring adventure, *Master and Commander*, he played Hogg the whaler, alongside the famously temperamental New Zealand Oscar-winner Russell Crowe. I don't know if they ever discussed their Wrexham connection, though – Crowe's grandfather, John Crowe, was a well-known fruit-and-veg wholesaler in the town.[9] Jones does play roles other than action heroes as well, of course, but his physique and craggy features mean he's a natural for authority figures, thuggish siblings and general tough guys.

Which is not what happens to Stifyn Parri, a Rhos acting export better known for the kiss than the punch. At Ysgol Morgan Llwyd, where rock operas were a yearly ritual, Stifyn was already displaying the flamboyant taste for the stage which brought him a career in musical theatre and television. He spent some years with the Liverpool soap opera *Brookside*, which saw him score another first for Wales' biggest village - the first gay kiss in a UK soap. He's made quite a career of the kiss, in one way or another. As a producer and impresario, and a dedicated friend of celebrities such as Shirley Bassey, Siân Lloyd and Catherine Zeta Jones, he set up a club for Welsh expatriates in London called SWS. The word 'sws' is Welsh for 'kiss', and is also an acronym for 'Social Welsh and Sexy'. Some unkinder commentators, however, had suggested it stood for 'Sad Welsh Sods'. Or even 'Sex With Sheep'. Now that would be a first for a UK soap.

But when it comes to firsts, Rhos has one undoubted world-beater – the first-ever British Miss World. It was 1961 when Rosemarie Frankland, brought up in Gornel, Rhos, won the Miss United Kingdom competition and then, in London, the Miss World contest,[10] where she was crowned by the comedian Bob Hope (whose mother was from Barry). In the wake of her triumph, Rosemarie returned to visit Rhos, where, despite her having moved to Lancashire when she was a girl, she still had many relatives. A photograph shows Rosemarie, in beehive hairdo, short white jacket, tight trousers and white ankle boots, alongside her grandmother, Fanny Green, a solid figure in floral pinny and sensible shoes.

During that visit, Bob Hope telephoned – not an easy task in 1961 when the only phone was in the local pub – to invite Rosemarie to join him on a worldwide tour of US army bases. She accepted, and later settled in the USA where she married and had a family. But she remained a Rhos girl, and after her untimely death at the age of fifty-seven in Marina del Ray near Los Angeles in 2000, her ashes were flown back to Wales to be interred in her grandmother's grave. When I visited the cemetery, I asked a couple tending a nearby grave if they could show me where Rosemarie was buried. They took me there. They'd been in school with her. "Oh, she was lovely. So lovely," the lady says. We look down at the grave. "She loved her grandmother, she did." The grave makes no mention of Rosemarie's achievements. She lies alongside the colliers, shopkeepers and housewives of Rhosllannerchrugog – reputedly Wales' biggest village, and definitely the final resting place of the world's most beautiful woman.

CEFN MAWR

Plas Madoc leisure centre is a giant blue box, with the words '*Sblasio*' and 'Run' scribbled across its front in ten-foot-high letters. Serving an estate of 1700 people, plus the surrounding area of Cefn Mawr and Ruabon, it's Wrexham's biggest leisure centre. Once state-of-the-art, and with its own 'tropical' pool, the centre is now, according to the council, 'reaching the end of its beneficial life'.

Some parts of Cefn Mawr seem to have reached the end of their beneficial life some time ago. Once, sustained by the income from coal and heavy industry, Cefn's redbrick main street had sixty-odd shops of every description, from jewellers to drapers to electrical goods; it even had its own cinemas and weekly newspaper. It was a self-contained world. Now, the mines have gone, and although the giant Flexsys chemical plant over the hill at Acrefair still employs hundreds, the area's industrial heyday has passed. Entire terraces of shops have gone, and others are boarded up, resigned to their fate. Where the demolished buildings stood, the ground stays empty and overgrown, nature providing the only infill development, reclaiming the land from the brief couple-of-centuries tenure of industry.

I had come here to visit the artist, Malcolm Hughes. I first came across his paintings about fifteen years ago in a second-hand bookshop in the People's Market in Wrexham town centre.[11] They were dark canvases and charcoals of the mining communities around Wrexham. I was instantly intrigued. Welsh landscape painting has some favourite territories, but Wrexham isn't one of them. I sometimes think there are more artists painting south Wales mining valley scenes than there were ever miners in the valleys; and every west Wales town and village that can snare a tourist seems to have its collection of galleries peddling picturesque views of Snowdonia, or of postcardy farms and cottages. But for the industrial communities of the north east, there's nothing. Even Ruabon-born Will Roberts, one of the greatest Welsh painters of the twentieth century, spent his life

in Neath in south Wales, his family having moved there when he was eleven. But these paintings in the bookshop were different. At last, someone was turning communities like my own home village into works of art. The only problem was, I couldn't afford them.

Years later, when I *could* afford them, I went back. The paintings were no longer on display, but the owner put us in touch, and a day or so later,

I was in Malcolm Hughes'
house on the Plas Madoc
estate, choosing from his
selection of paintings of
Ruabon, Cefn Mawr and
Wrexham. They're intense
monochrome studies com-
posed of brick walls, shadows,
chapels, memorial plaques,
clouds, rooftops, windows,
doorways, rusting iron rail-
ings, stunted trees, gable ends,
pavements, gutters and hill-
sides. I have four of them in
my study. I may not live in Wrexham any more, but when I work, I
surround myself with these charcoal reminders of home.

Malcolm's a self-effacing type; exhibits rarely, sells only when
persuaded. His house in Plas Madoc is stacked with books and
periodicals. In between the works of cultural theorists, Welsh poets,
English historians and Russian novelists, are the cages of the
injured wild birds Malcolm nurses back to health. Whenever we
talk, he doesn't want to say much about his own work, but he never
fails to tell me about his personal hero, the great 'lost' Welsh painter
Wynne Lewis. A Coedpoeth man whose father died in the
Gresford disaster, Lewis himself served in the Second World War,
and never forgot the sight of the destruction in Germany. He married a German woman, and returned to Britain, winning a place at
the Slade School of Fine Art where he became a rising star of the
Euston Road School of painters, a group opposed to *avant-garde*
styles and dedicated to socially-relevant realism.

Then Lewis' promising career was blighted by an accidental head
injury. He became increasingly eccentric. His wife returned to Germany
with their young daughter Isobel, and Lewis stayed in his Coedpoeth
council house, painting. Endlessly painting: interiors, still lives, and the
landscapes around Coedpoeth. Influenced by Catholic artists like David
Jones, with whom he corresponded, he used the villages of Coedpoeth,
Minera and New Brighton as backgrounds for scenes of the
Crucifixion. But he never exhibited, and he never tried to sell anything.
His house was bare of furniture apart from a table and chairs, and a
mattress on the floor; sacks were nailed over the windows, and candles
were the only light. When Lewis made tea for his occasional visitors, he

served it an old salmon tin.

Only once did he ever sell a piece of work, to his friend Tom Ellis, the MP, when he was short of cash. It's a still life in the style of Cezanne, and is now on display in Tom Ellis' home; as far as anyone knows, it's the only one of Lewis' paintings to be preserved. In his Welsh-language autobiography,[12] Ellis recalls intervening, a few years later, in a dispute with Wrexham council, who were threatening to evict Lewis for non-payment of rent. The MP contacted the Slade and spoke to its director, Sir William Coldstream, who immediately agreed to use a charity fund not just to pay Lewis' arrears but to pay his rent for the rest of his life. Asked by Tom Ellis why the offer was so generous, Sir William's reply was unhesitating: "You must appreciate," he said. "He is one of the most significant British painters this century."

However, due to Lewis' own hermit-like existence, that significance remained unrecognised. When Lewis died in the 1990s, Wrexham council's former arts officer Steve Brake visited the house in the Adwy to make sure the paintings were saved. It was too late. Lewis had done most of his work on paper, and in the neglected house the paintings were rotting. Only a handful survived, going to Lewis' daughter who came over from Germany. But later attempts to contact her to ensure the paintings are exhibited have failed.[13] All that remains is the one painting kept by Tom Ellis, and the sketches Malcolm Hughes made of the interior of Lewis' home, the council house where the great Welsh artist's work went through the entire life cycle from conception to destruction, unseen, unsung and unsold.

Unforgotten, too, for Malcolm. The loss haunts him. He shows me his sketches of Lewis' house; in which Lewis is always shown surrounded by his works, but with his back to the viewer, looking away. "If you had seen the paintings... Magnificent studies of Coedpoeth and Minera. You could see the European influences in his work; you could see the great thought. Wynne had the talent and the perception to be thought of as one of the great European painters. He had that talent. There are good Welsh painters, but Wynne went beyond. He seemed to grasp the essence..."

Malcolm's paintings grasp the essence of the industrial districts of Wrexham for me. He shows me around these communities of Cefn Mawr, Acrefair, Trevor and Pontcysyllte, which once set the pace for the rest of the industrial world. It was here in 1805 that Thomas Telford built the Pontcysyllte aquaduct, a state-of-the-art cast-iron river one hundred and twenty feet above the Dee Valley, an engineering marvel in its day; the novelist Sir Walter Scott called it the finest work of art he had ever seen. Two centuries later, it's still carrying canal traffic. It was here too that Robert Graesser, later to found the Wrexham Lager business, discovered a way of making oil from shale and, in 1867, established a chemical works at Acrefair, turning the site into the world's leading producer of phenols, employing two thousand people and making the area a byword for its pungent atmosphere. The smell has gone, but so are most of the jobs.[14]

Graesser's former house is one of the more impressive buildings in Cefn Mawr, sited on a hillside overlooking the Dee Valley. All of Cefn Mawr is on a hillside in one way or another, and the whole settlement is intersected with footpaths and lanes which provide vertical shortcuts between the horizontal roads. Malcolm strides up the steepest without losing breath. He and his wife have a mountain smallholding, so these hills are nothing to him. We reach the very top of Cefn. Here, Malcolm tells me, was a house owned by a local man who kept a private library in the cellar. When he moved away, and the house was earmarked for demolition, he told Malcolm he could take any books he wanted. He went there, but too late. The demolition men had collapsed the house onto its foundations, burying the cellar and its volumes under the mound of rubble. It's still there, under the summit of Cefn, a bibliophile's burial mound, the entombed tomes a treasure trove for some future archaeologist to unearth.

We go back towards the village centre. Here, in the park, are the remains of Plas Kynaston, an early sixteenth century gentry house of the Kynaston family. It's had many uses, including a stint as the local library. Now, the core of the building, with its double-gabled frontage, is closed up. A couple of styrofoam chip containers lie on the steps.

Nearby, a billboard from the Cefn Mawr Townscape Heritage Initiative advertises the urban renewal planned for the village. It's going to start with the former Ebenezer Chapel. Opposite the Cymru Kebab House, the old place of worship is being transformed. A tall, toughened-glass atrium is being bolted to the end. It will be a community space, enterprise centre and coffee shop, with a piazza outside. It's costing three and a half million pounds from the Welsh Assembly Government, the Welsh Development Agency, Cadw, and the Heritage Lottery. For some, it's a foretaste of regeneration; to others it's a vandal-doomed white elephant. The sign says: "Boasting a continental-style pavement cafe, the Cefn Square will set the standards for the area, attracting visitors and bringing new life to the commercial centre." The

artist's impression shows people sitting outside as though in the Piazza San Marco. Continental cafe culture for Cefn. It's not yet a subject for a Canaletto. But there will be a place for a cappuccino. It's a start.

RUABON. RED BRICK, BLUE BLOOD

The term 'painting the town red' might have been invented for Ruabon. This place is responsible for more red in more towns than anywhere you care to name. It's been a major centre of distinctive red tile and brick-making since 1878, when huge deposits of high-quality Etruria Marl clay were discovered here, and when Henry Dennis established the giant Hafod Red Brick Works to exploit them. From the works at Ruabon and nearby Abenbury came the hard, glazed red bricks which are the main building material of many parts of Wrexham and the surrounding area, as well as many places further afield. Ruabon Brick was bold, assertive, plentiful and long-lasting, and the Victorians couldn't get enough of it. It symbolised the power of the new industrial middle-classes.

It was Ruabon which gave the world the adjective 'redbrick' to describe the new universities which were built in the industrial cities of Britain as power gradually moved from the elite centres of Oxford and Cambridge to the emerging provincial bourgeoisie. The term comes from the work of a don at Liverpool University, Edgar Allison Peers, whose 1943 book *Redbrick University*, examined the phenomenon of the new learning institutions. He was referring to the ornate Victoria Building at Liverpool University, built in 1892 by Alfred

Waterhouse out of Ruabon brick and terracotta. The Victoria Building, whose Welsh-made construction material became a worldwide shorthand for meritocratic higher education, was a centrepiece of Liverpool's activities in 2008, as European Capital of Culture.

Ruabon brick has left its mark in the capital of Wales too. At the turn of the twentieth century, Ruabon produced the huge terracotta murals for the side of Cardiff's redbrick Pier Head Building, now part of the National Assembly complex. And around ninety years later, the same material was used for the specially-commissioned maritime-themed sculptured benches ranged around the seat of Welsh government. On the back of the paviers which form the entrance to the National Assembly building are two words: 'Dennis Ruabon'.

And in Bute Park behind Cardiff Castle, I once found another intriguing connection. In the gardens near the gorsedd circle is the cruciform floor of a church, complete with tiles and memorial plaques. The walls, at a uniform height of a couple of feet, were built out of bricks marked 'Dennis Ruabon.' I found this connection with my home area rather poignant, and it inspired a sonnet about this ruined place of worship made from materials from north east Wales.

Later I began to have my doubts. On closer inspection, I realised the grave in the centre of the church was medieval, and the huge tree whose branches were growing into the empty nave must be centuries old. How could such an old structure have been made out of Victorian materials? The poet Peter Finch, series editor of the *Real* books, and obsessive chronicler of Cardiff's past and present, gave me the answer. The church is a medieval Benedictine monastery, destroyed by Owain Glyndŵr, derelict for centuries, and then, in the nineteenth century, tidied up by the coal magnate and antiquarian, the Marquess of Bute. He had its outline picked out with a few courses of the building material of the day – Ruabon brick. So that explained it. A pity I'd already published the poem.

Clay, coal and iron formed the modern settlement of Ruabon during the industrial revolution. It was already noted for its industry when George Borrow visited in the 1850s. When he asked a local woman the name of a ridge on the skyline, he was delighted to be greeted with '*Dim Saesneg*' ('No English'), and he said to himself: "This is as it should be. I now feel I am in Wales."[15] However, the settlement itself is much older than the age of industry, with evidence of Bronze and Iron Age occupation. The village's name comes from the Welsh word *rhiw*, meaning 'hill', and the personal name Mabon, possibly the name of a sixth century saint who may have founded the village's original church. The current church, St Mary's, dates from the fourteenth century and is on the foundation of the older building. It's an important medieval structure and it has one of Wales' best memorial effigies, showing John ap Elis Eyton and Elizabeth Calverly who died in 1526 and 1524 respectively.[16]

This aristocratic connection was responsible for the other aspect of Ruabon's dual heritage. It's ironic that this village which was one of the most important industrial centres of Wales was also the home of one of its most powerful aristocratic families. The connection goes back at least to the Wars of the Roses when John ap Elis Eyton was granted lands at Ruabon as a reward for his support of Henry Tudor at Bosworth. These estates were inherited in 1718 by the Wynn family, descendants of the Welsh princes, and founders of the Williams-Wynn dynasty. From their home at Wynnstay Hall[17] on the hillside opposite Ruabon, successive Sir Watkinses dominated local and north Wales affairs, for more than two hundred years. The fifth baronet was so powerful he was given the only-partly-ironic title of 'The Prince of Wales'. And as for the sixth baronet, his coming-of-age in 1841 was celebrated with three days of celebrations and feasting on an epic, Biblical scale. The week's gargantuan food bill featured items such as: 21 Oxen; 26 Sets of Calves' Feet; 829 Bottles of Sherry; 558 Bottles of Port; 294 Bottles of Claret; 336 Bottles of Champagne; 56 Bottles of Madeira, and flitches and bushels and hogsheads galore.[18]

The Williams Wynns enjoyed all the trappings of the super rich: a splendid London town house, a personal Welsh triple-harpist (Blind John Parry of Ruabon), and even, at one stage a private regiment, the Ancient British Fencible Cavalry.[19] They moved at the highest levels of European society, as can be seen in the diaries of the *Diaries of a Lady of Quality*[20] written between 1797 and 1844 by Miss Frances Williams Wynn, the daughter of Sir Watkin Williams Wynn, the fourth baronet, where gossip, sensations and ghost stories alternate with intimate anecdotes of statesmen, princes and monarchs. Frances is enjoying a belated celebrity as a posthumous blogger thanks to the feminist commentator Natalie Bennett[21] who's been posting up successive entries from Frances' diaries on a special website.[22]

But blue blood eventually had to yield to red brick. The Williams Wynns and their kind could only thrive while feudal conditions of patronage survived. However much they may have fed porkers to the proles on great occasions, and however much they may have been patrons of the arts, their power had a dark side, which they weren't averse to using. One Sir Watkin evicted the mother of the nonconformist minister Michael D. Jones from her home. This injustice inspired Jones to find a haven for Welsh nonconformists free from the stranglehold of landowner and church, leading him to establish the Welsh colony in Patagonia, eight thousand miles away from the high-handed aristocrats of north Wales. However, emigration wasn't an option for the majority. They stayed home, remembered their grievances, and gathered their strength. As the industrial classes of Britain grew, and demanded education, rights and political power, the days of the great houses were numbered. Democracy had quietly undermined them like the colliery workings under the Wynnstay's lush Capability Brown parkland, and by the middle of the twentieth century, the end had come. Death duties fragmented the estates, and in 1947, forced the Williams Wynns to sell their showpiece, Wynnstay itself.[23] It later became a private school, which itself went bust in 1994. After a period empty, it's now luxury apartments, on 999-year leases, for the new ruling class.

THE HOME OF WELSH FOOTBALL

As the old aristocracy were declining, a new one was arising. The place which was the home of the last great feudal family of Wales is also the birthplace of Welsh international football, and of some of its greatest players.

In terms of Welsh soccer, Ruabon is the cradle of civilisation. A mile up the road is the place where the first football club in Wales was formed – Plasmadoc FC, in 1869, which three years later became the Druids. Trying to work out the exact origins of the club is rather like trying to determine the origins of the ancient druids themselves. But from the swirling mists of football's Victorian prehistory, it's 'The Ancients', as the Welsh club are called, who emerge with the best claim to be the originals. Original and best they were for quite a while too, winning the Welsh Cup eight times between 1880 and 1904. The club's name has gone through numerous changes since then, due to mergers and, in recent years, the inclusion of the names of sponsoring organisations. But the 'Druids' element remains, and the team, as 'NEWI Cefn Druids,' and currently managed by legendary former Wrexham striker Dixie McNeil, now plays in the Welsh Premier League, entertaining the likes of Connahs Quay Nomads and Bangor City to its ground at Plas Kynaston Lane (capacity two thousand, seats three hundred) in Cefn Mawr, which they have occupied since 1961.

Although it's not exactly the Millennium Stadium, the facilities at Plas Kynaston Lane are better than those of many Welsh Premier League teams, and they give the club a distinct advantage. As a national league, the Welsh Premier's best teams qualify for Europe, and, as European football rules require clubs to have a minimum standard of ground facilities, the Druids can qualify even if they finish lower down the league than other clubs with inferior facilities. The club's facilities are likely to improve further if, as planned, they move to a new site nearby when their current ground is sold to Tesco.

It was only a matter of some six years after the formation of Plasmadoc FC, that Wales decided it needed its own international football association. Ruabon is where it happened. It was at the Wynnstay Hotel here in February 1876 that a group of local businessmen formed the Football Association of Wales. The catalyst was a local solicitor called Llewelyn Kenrick, who was a keen member of Druids, and quite a useful full-back himself.[24] The group's main aim was to form a Welsh side to challenge Scotland, who had begun playing internationals with England about four years earlier. The newly-formed Welsh team lost its first fixture, with the Scots, in March that year, by four goals to nil, but by 1881, they were good enough to beat England, a feat which they managed by one goal to nil at Blackburn, on 26 February. *The Wrexham Advertiser* recorded the great event, at a time when soccer reporting was in its infancy:

> Hawtrey, the English goalkeeper, threw the ball out but was charged over at the same time and Vaughan running up placed the leather safely through the goal for Wales. The Englishmen strove hard to get on terms with their opponents. Shot after shot was aimed at the Welsh goal but each attempt was rendered futile. When time was called Wales were declared winners by one goal to love.[25]

Wales may well have later been eclipsed by newer soccer nations, but there's a lot to be said for getting in at the ground floor, and the nation enjoys a lasting legacy from being the third oldest football association in the world (after England and Scotland). It's a permanent member of the International Football Association Board (IFAB), the body which actually makes the rules for association football worldwide. Formed in 1886, its membership is made up of one representative of each of the four British nations, and four representatives of FIFA, the sport's organising body. In football terms, this is the equivalent of the United Nations Security Council, and Wales is a permanent member. In this, if nothing else, Wales is a superpower.

And Wales gave the world its first footballing superstar too. Billy Meredith. Born in 1874 to a mining family at Black Park near Chirk, he worked as a miner before his football skills brought him a career on the turf rather than under it. He played for Chirk, won a Welsh Cup winner's medal, and played briefly for Wrexham before going over the border to England where he quickly made a name for himself as a mercurial winger, known as the 'Welsh Wizard', or sometimes 'The Wizard of Dribble'.[26] He captained Manchester City to an F.A. Cup victory in 1904, bounced back from a damaging bribery allegation and joined Manchester United, with whom he won two league championships and another F.A.Cup medal. He ended his career back with City, and was the oldest player ever to play international football – turning out for Wales for the last of his forty-eight appearances for his country at the age of forty-five and two hundred and twenty-nine days. Meredith's influence also stretched beyond the pitch, as he led the fight for players' rights and proper pay, a fact recognised by the Professional Footballers' Association more than half a century after his death in 1958 at the age of eighty-four, when they clubbed together with the Welsh FA, Manchester City and Manchester United, to put a proper headstone on his previously unmarked grave in Manchester's Southern Cemetery (plot number Y760). The new stone was unveiled by his ninety-four-year-old daughter Winifred.[27]

Ruabon produced one of Wales' greatest modern footballers too, Mark 'Sparky' Hughes, who was born in the village in 1963. His great grandfather used to keep the Queen's Head Hotel in nearby Cefn Mawr. Hughes started his football career at the top and has stayed there ever since as player and manager. He signed for Manchester United straight from school in 1980, winning the FA Cup with them in 1985 before joining Barcelona, then Bayern Munich, and returning to United in 1988. Over the next seven years at Old Trafford, Hughes' goal-scoring skills contributed to two League Championships, two FA Cup victories, and one victory each in the League Cup and the 1991 European Cup Winners' Cup, in which he scored both United goals in the final 2-1 triumph. His later career took him to Chelsea, Southampton, Everton, and Blackburn, where he finished his playing days and became manager, and where he's currently contracted until 2009. He also managed Wales for five years, narrowly missing out on qualification for the European Championships in 2004 in one of those agonising hair's-breadth last-minute failures which all Welsh international soccer fans experience every four years or so as though they were part of some painful but inevitable natural cycle.

WRITERS

The author and Ruabon old-boy Frank Harris liked to score too. His exploits, however, were confined to the bedroom, and, to a certain degree, to his imagination. He was born in Galway in Ireland in 1865 to Welsh parents. But at the age of twelve, he was sent as a boarder to Ruabon's historic grammar school, founded in the early seventeenth century and one of the oldest educational establishments in Wales.[28]

Harris hated it. At the time, Ruabon practised a rigid system of chiefs, monitors, sub-monitors, and fagging, in which younger boys were the servants of older ones, both domestically and – thanks to the code of silence which ruled the dormitories – sexually.

> If the mothers of England knew what goes on in the dormitories of these boarding-schools throughout England, they would all be closed, from Eton and Harrow upwards or downwards, in a day. If English fathers even had brains enough to see that the fires of sex need no stoking in boyhood, they too would prevent their sons from the foul abuse.[29]

Ruabon was 'England' as far as Harris was concerned. When he records a trip to Rhyl, and the obligatory precocious sexual adventure, he describes the location as being 'in North Wales'. But whether Wales or England, Harris felt like a 'caged bird' at Ruabon, and, as an escape from the discipline, he immersed himself in the school library, filling his head with stories of adventures in the Wild West. He finally managed to escape in 1870 when he won fifteen pounds in a composition contest and used the money to get to Liverpool and book himself on a transatlantic steamer, lying to the company about his age.[30]

After a time as a cowboy, he became a writer, and was a precocious, pugnacious and influential editor of periodicals on both sides
of the Atlantic, counting people like Oscar Wilde, H.G.Wells, James
Thurber, Bram Stoker and George Bernard Shaw among his circle of
friends and, in the 1920s, sharing a house with the occultist Aleister
Crowley. He courted controversy. Wilde said Harris had been
received in all the great houses of London – once. "He blazed
through London like a comet, leaving a trail of deeply annoyed per-
sons behind him," said Shaw. Harris had literary ambitions, and
wrote biographies, plays and short stories, but his ambition out-
stripped his ability, and the only work of his which is still read at all
widely is his own 1922 autobiography *My Life and Loves,* in which he
gleefully detailed his claimed sexual encounters – "Casanova! My
dear man, Casanova is not worthy to untie my bootstrings," – and in
which he helpfully included nude photographs of women, supposedly his conquests, but possibly just put there to help the book sell.
Whatever, it worked. The book was a *succès de scandale,* achieving the
rare distinction of being banned even in Paris. Both its accuracy and
its literary merit have been questioned. Harris himself, though, was
undeterred. If people didn't appreciate his work, it was their fault: "I
am, really, a great writer," he said. "My only difficulty is finding great
readers."[31] Self-confidence wasn't a problem for Harris. He concluded his memoirs by reflecting on his approaching death and con-
soling himself with the fact that future generations would count him
a genius:

> 'He has written naughty passages', says one, and my friend replies 'so
> did Shakespeare in *Hamlet* and with less provocation'. 'His life is the
> fullest ever lived', says my disciple, and they all stand shocked, for this
> is plainly the truth and they all realize that a supreme word has been
> spoken and that such a man is among the great forever.[32]

On the top shelf, forever, certainly. Harris' work is a classic of
period erotica, and is available from numerous specialist bookshops
and websites. Although the curious need not resort to the back alleys
to find it: I got my copy from Cardiff Central Library where it was
handed over with a matter-of-fact air which Harris would, I'm sure,
have found vaguely disappointing.

Errata.
(My Life and Loves Volume II, Frank Harris, 1925)

p8 'youg' for young
p15 'inconccivably' for inconceivably
p30 'Bessy' for Bessie
p76 'honseless' ought to be houseless
p127 'overton' ought to be 'Ovington'
p179 Homosexualist, not homsexualist
p279 Delete comma after 'maiden'
p298 'Tock' should be took
p356 'Drived' should be drivel
p358 'Bushed' should be hushed
p373 'Nuissances' should be nuisances
p377 'Deadfully' should be dreadfully
p394 A colon after 'twitched' should be a comma
p412 'Temtation' should be temptation

Harris wrote much, travelled widely and achieved little of lasting value in literary terms. Another writer who lived at Ruabon wrote little, travelled less, but achieved a great deal.

On the west side of the village is a tree-lined close of semi-detached houses called Vicarage Fields. For many years, this was the home of the poet Bryan Martin Davies, one of the most important voices in Welsh-language poetry of the last third of the twentieth century, and the person responsible for my own decision to pursue a literary path.

I met him in 1980 when I'd left Ysgol Morgan Llwyd and had started studying at Yale Sixth Form College. As Morgan Llwyd had its own sixth form, it was unusual for anyone from there to attend Yale, but I did so, partly because my brother had gone there, and partly because I wanted to study economics, which wasn't available at Morgan Llwyd. As a Welsh speaker, I therefore found myself in an instant tiny minority, and even though in the past I'd rebelled against Morgan Llwyd's Welsh-language orthodoxy and was glad to leave for broader horizons, I now found out just how important the language was to my identity, and quickly rebelled myself back into solidarity with my native culture. It was at this crucial point of self-discovery that I met Bryan Martin Davies.

He was the Welsh lecturer at Yale, and although I wasn't studying Welsh, I did happen to be in his registration class, where the fact that we had the language in common created a connection. A gruff, saturnine figure, he was the first South Walian I had ever met, and the first poet. One day, after registration, he asked me, in his tobacco-roughened voice, whether I wrote. I had no idea quite how important a literary figure he was, but I duly showed him the juvenile attempts I was producing in English at that time. He encouraged me to write in Welsh, and over the two years at Yale, and the years that followed, I served a kind of informal apprenticeship as he gradually taught me the essentials of the poet's craft.

And more than the craft. You can learn how to avoid clichés; how to string together a coherent sequence of metaphors on a particular theme; how to write in images rather than with adjectives. But more important is the development of the faculty of perception; of opening yourself up to experience so that scenes, situations and feelings can find their expression through you. I hardly understood what he meant when he tried to cultivate that quality in me. But I tried. By this time, poetry was far more important to me than my studies, and I was missing geography lessons wholesale in order to encounter nature and the land at first-hand. I recall standing for hours one December morning in a deserted snow-covered meadow at Pantywyll, trying to force the senses to interpret the blinding beauty of the scene as it deserved. Those innumerable sparkling points where the sun hit the hard crust of the snow. Diamonds? Teardrops? Ground glass? My words always fell short.

One night, I had stayed up Minera Mountain until it had gone dark; I could see the glowing fires of Brymbo Steelworks just over the next hill, and beyond that the black expanse of Maelor and the Cheshire Plain, scattered with pinpoints of lights pulsing quietly through the distorting filter of the atmosphere. Embers? Signals? Moonlight on a dark sea? The horizon stretched away, endless, impassive, always with more distances than you could ever reach, always with more potential than you could ever fulfil, always with more experiences than you could ever name. And the realisation struck me like the cold night wind. This was going to *hurt*. Life was going to hurt. And the more you opened yourself up to it, the more you would suffer. I came down the mountain sobered and chilled.

The following day, I asked Bryan Martin, apprehensively: "Does a poet have to suffer?" I wanted to be a poet more than anything, but I was now wondering whether the price was worth paying. I can't remember his answer. Perhaps it was something enigmatic. But since then, I've had the opportunity to reflect on his own career, from the standpoint of having experienced a poetic journey of my own, and this has given me an idea of the answer. But let me say a little more about Bryan Martin's own career first.

He was born in 1933 and brought up in the mining village of
Brynaman in Carmarthenshire, and served his own poetic apprenticeship with J.M. Edwards of Barry and with Gwenallt, the great
Welsh poet who was his teacher at university in Aberystwyth. Bryan
Martin himself reached an early literary maturity, winning the
National Eisteddfod Crown two years running in 1970 and 1971
with free-verse poems whose intense imagery and hard-edged alliter-
ative quality indicated a new direction for poetry in Welsh. But from
the beginning, it was a vision in which the shadows were more apparent than the light: "the dark hell/that lurks only the thickness of a cig-
arette paper/the other side of our day."[33] The decaying, claustropho-
bic industrial valleys of his first volume *Darluniau ar Gynfas*
('Pictures on Canvas'), were superseded a few years later, when he
moved to Wrexham to work as a teacher, by the threatening, exposed,
conflicted borderlands of Offa's Dyke, which became, in his work, a
symbol of division, a psychic scar.

By the time of his latest volume, *Pan Oedd y Nos yn Wenfflam*
('When the Night was Blazing') in 1988, he had suffered badly
from cancer surgery, from the loss of his wife to multiple sclerosis,
and from depression. From the darkness of these experiences, he
re-entered, in his imagination, the blighted industrial landscapes of
his youth, and came back with an extended fable in which light is
eternally resurrected, even through the crucifixion of suffering. It's
his most profound and most achieved work, in which he answers
the troubling questions of his earlier volumes with a hard-won,
exhausted but conclusive optimism. Looking back over the last
three decades of his work, and thinking back to my own question
to Bryan Martin Davies in the early 1980s, "Does a poet have to
suffer?" I find it hard to avoid the conclusion that the answer, if
we're talking about poetry that goes to the heart of the human
experience, is "yes".

CHIRK

The road between Wrexham and Oswestry used to snake slowly
through the narrower parts of the Dee Valley, following the redbrick-
flanked contours of the villages of Rhostyllen, Johnstown, Ruabon
and Rhosymedre around the spurs of the Berwyn mountains. It
crossed first the Dee valley, and then the Ceiriog valley, next to
Thomas Telford's spectacular seventy-foot-tall Chirk aquaduct,[34] and

the accompanying one hundred-foot-tall railway viaduct,[35] which links Wales and England.

Now, for the last decade or so, the new A483 has straightened the line between the two border towns, aiming directly across the flatter lands to the east, transecting contour lines, truncating journey times, and soaring into England on a bridge higher than Thomas Telford would have thought possible, but routine for today's road-builders. On its way, like concrete flypaper, it's attracting gradual accretions of service stations, car boot sales, mobile snack bars and roadside eateries.

One of these is at Halton, a tiny collection of farms and some small-scale mineworkers' housing which was once a half-forgotten hamlet in the unfrequented borderland where Wales shades into England.[36] Now the main road thunders past a hundred yards or so to the west, and McDonald's have opened a drive-in restaurant. The Golden Arches look down on a little metal mission church, now a private house. This is one of the hundreds, if not thousands, of such buildings put up as Christianity's rapid response to the sudden growth of industrial communities all over Britain. Prefabricated off-the-peg prayer houses. Ready-made religion. Fast food for the faithful.

This particular outlet has a small place in history, as it's where the great priest-poet, Ronald Stuart Thomas (1913-2000) preached his first sermon. Brought up at Holyhead on Anglesey as the only child of an over-protective mother and an often-absent sea-captain father, R.S. Thomas had been studying for the priesthood at St Michael's College in Llandaff in Cardiff, but, reserved and shy, he had managed to duck out of the obligatory test-sermon during his training period. However, when he arrived for his first job as curate of Chirk in 1936,

he could evade his speaking duties no longer, and Halton was the site of the world preaching premiere of a man who would later be counted as one of the greatest religious poets in the English language ever.[37] In his 1985 autobiography, *Neb*, he says it was here he first encountered the problem of pain, as he saw the hardship of the mining families. Chirk parish was also where he met his wife, Mildred Eldridge, an

English artist. Thomas' vicar didn't approve of married curates, though, and the couple had to leave, with Thomas taking up the curacy of Tallarn Green near Hanmer, even closer to the English border. Halton's 'iron church', as it's known locally, now has solar panels and a barrel to collect rainwater, two things of which the nature-loving Thomas would have approved. What he would have thought of the

neighbouring McDonald's, though, doesn't bear thinking about.

Chirk[38] itself is a pleasant little place with a medieval, partly Norman, church. It's quiet, much more so than in the past, now that most traffic is diverted to the bypass. One constant element of traffic here, though, is the regular stream of log lorries heading to the giant Kronospan wood processing plant, a steaming complex of silver metal occupying a hundred-acre site on the edge of the village. It's the third biggest MDF-manufacturing plant in the world, and employs six hundred and seventy people, nearly all local. This is industry as it used to be: a huge integrated enterprise with its own forests, railway station and sawmill. Private plantations in Scotland send logs by special train, feeding the plant's appetite for a million and a half tonnes of raw material per year, to be turned into MDF, HDF, OSB, T&G[39] flooring, chipboard, kitchen worktops, storage pallets and laminate. Every year, fifty thousand timber deliveries arrive by road and rail. The worktop in your kitchen; your office desk, there's a good chance it was made here. The log lorry you're stuck behind on a winding road in mid Wales; it'll almost certainly be on its way to Chirk.

The factory's white plume is visible from tens of miles away, an unmistakeable vaporous landmark. The area's other major landmark is Chirk Castle, on a hill close by. This is one of the castles built to subdue the Welsh in the wake of the defeat of Llywelyn the Last by Edward I in 1282, and, unique among the castles of the conquest, is still occupied today. It was built in 1295 by Roger Mortimer, one of the Marcher Lords to whom Edward delegated the job of keeping the defeated Welsh in check. It saw action in the English Civil War, when it was besieged and taken by the forces of Parliament, although it was given back to its owners at the Restoration. The last aristocratic family to own it, the Myddletons, eventually gifted it to the National Trust.[40] The Myddletons themselves are descendants of Rhirid Flaidd, a twelfth century Welsh prince who traced his own descent from Cunedda Wledig, the sixth century Celtic King of Cumbria, one of the last-surviving Celtic kingdoms in what is now England.

Despite being founded as a means of suppressing Welsh identity, Chirk Castle, like so many other institutions of its kind, ancient and modern, has found itself unable to resist the gradual influence of the native culture, seeping in slowly like moisture through its stones.[41] In the early sixteenth century, Chirk Castle's Constable was Wiliam ap Siôn Edwart (d. 1532) He was a typical renaissance man with the obligatory, and seemingly exhausting, CV the age seemed to require: huntsman, soldier, musician, genealogist, and patron.[42] He kept close contact with the court of Henry VIII and fought in the siege of Tournai, when Henry captured the only Belgian city ever to be ruled by a British king. But as well as his continental adventures, Wiliam also kept in touch with his native culture and was a noted patron of Welsh poets after he was made constable of Chirk by Henry in 1526.[43]

Four centuries later, Chirk Castle was again home to a renaissance man. Thomas Evelyn Scott-Ellis, the eighth Baron Howard de Walden and the fourth Baron Seaford (1880-1946). He had been born in London, but his parents were Welsh, descendants of an old Wrexham family who had made their money in the West Indies. He inherited the Howard title through the female line, and made his home in Chirk Castle in 1912, quickly learning Welsh and becoming a persuasive proponent of the old language and of Welsh culture.

At the same time, he kept a close connection with fashionable London society – being deeply involved with the Haymarket Theatre and becoming a trustee of the Tate Gallery. In Wales, in the mid-1930s he became the first secretary of the Contemporary Art Society for Wales. He was described as:

> ... a reticent grandee and polymath, a man of great wealth and estates, a figure in society, accomplished sportsman and traveller. He was also a poet and lavish patron of the arts.[44]

No mean poet, either, as can be seen for the gutsy libretti he wrote for three operas by the popular contemporary composer Joseph Holbrooke. The trilogy, a kind of Welsh Wagnerian conception based on Celtic myth, was called *The Cauldron of Annwn*. Well-received in its day, it's almost totally forgotten now.[45]

However, it may have left its mark in an unexpected way. One of the operas, based on the story of Dylan eil Don, the mythical *Mabinogion* figure, was entitled *Dylan, Son of the Wave*. It premiered in 1914, to enthusiastic reviews, and it's thought that the sudden vogue given to this ancient Welsh name encouraged Dylan Thomas' father to choose that name for his son, born that year. That apparently stern schoolmaster, Thomas senior, was perhaps as susceptible to the vagaries of fashion as any modern parent who calls their child 'Cruz' or 'Keira'.[46]

Howard de Walden's career as a patron of arts and poets was so long-lived, that he later became one of the first to encourage the talent of the young Dylan Thomas, in the 1930s. In due course, Thomas himself visited the Llangollen area, when he spent some time at the eisteddfod in 1953, writing a famous description:

> Here, over the bridge, come three Javanese, winged, breastplated, hel-meted, carrying gongs and steel bubbles. Kilted, sporraned, tartan'd, daggered Scotsmen, reel and strathspey up a side street, piping hot. Burgundian girls, wearing, on their heads, bird-cages made of velvet, suddenly whisk on the pavement into a coloured dance. A Viking goes into a pub. In black felt feathered hats and short leather trousers, enormous Austrians, with thighs big as Welshmen's bodies, but much browner, yodel to fiddles and split the rain with their smiles. Frilled, ribboned, sashed, fezzed, and white-turbaned, in baggy-blue shar-avari and squashed red boots, Ukrainians with Manchester accents gopack up the hill. Everything is strange in Llangollen. You wish you had a scarlet hat, and bangles, and a little bagpipe to call your own.

That passage shows Thomas using many of his favourite tech-niques: fusing words together with hyphens to make new hybrid descriptions, pressing nouns into service as verbs and/or adjectives as prodigally as if there was no tomorrow. There wasn't much of a tomorrow for Thomas. Four months later, thanks to an alcoholic binge in New York, he was dead.

He probably won't be the last dissolute Welsh poet to die in America. He certainly wasn't the first. A mile or so from Glyn Ceiriog is the village of Selattyn – the Welsh name belies the fact that it's now just over the border in Shropshire – which is where Goronwy Owen was curate from 1748 to 1753. Goronwy was the great hope of eighteenth century Welsh letters; a gifted poet and classical scholar born in humble circumstances in Anglesey in 1723, taken up by influential neo-classicist patrons, and primed to restore

the lost glories of Welsh poetry. Perhaps the expectations were too much for him. Boozy and quarrelsome, he lurched from crisis to crisis; tragedies, disappointments and scandals following him everywhere, even when he emigrated to Virginia to work as a lecturer in the College of William and Mary. There, he joined a student riot and was disgraced. Only in his last years did he find a measure of tranquillity, as a tobacco farmer in Brunswick County. He wrote only one poem during his 12-year exile, a poignant elegy for his patron, Lewis Morris, laced with grief and *hiraeth*. He died in 1769 aged 46 and was buried on his plantation. The College of William and Mary still remembers him, though – it has a small library collection dedicated to him, and a wood-panelled lecture theatre which is kept just as it was when he taught there.[47] And literary pilgrims trek to the site of his farm to look at his reputed grave, in the heat-hazed, cricket-chirping Virginia countryside of the American South, an ocean away from Wales.

GLYN CEIRIOG

Glyn Ceiriog is Wrexham's Wild West, a panhandle of mid Wales territory lassoed by the creators of local-government boundaries and hitched on to the largely-industrial and mercantile bulk of the borough. It's a twisting, inaccessible valley reaching deep into the Berwyn mountains, and its river, the Ceiriog, is reputed to be the fastest-flowing in Wales. It's the most scenic part of Wrexham borough, although most of the borough's residents have hardly heard of it, let alone been there.

This is partly because of Glyn Ceiriog's remoteness, and the fact that it isn't on the road to anywhere. Even though I knew many people from there, I'd never previously ventured further than Pontfadog, about halfway up the valley, and then only once. But one thing I did know: Glyn Ceiriog was different.

I remember many children from Glyn Ceiriog at Ysgol Morgan

Llwyd. They had a slightly exotic air compared to the townies and the children from industrial villages who made up the bulk of the school's population. They not only spoke Welsh, but thought in Welsh. For many of us, although we could speak the old language, it was English which was our *lingua franca* and our reflex language, the tongue to which we reverted at times of stress. Not so the kids from Glyn Ceiriog. I remember one of them, a rugby team-mate, being sent off for 'swearing' by a monoglot ref who was convinced – wrongly – that the gutteral sounds he had heard emanating from a ruck could only have been expletives. The Glyn Ceiriog kids had their own social circle. They went home early when it snowed. They had time off to help with the harvest. They had an air of independence the rest of us lacked.

My guide for my visit was the poet and novelist Elin Llwyd Morgan. Although not a native of the valley, she's lived there for more than ten years with her partner, Peris, one of my school contemporaries, and a member of one of the valley's most prominent families. I knew Elin through having included some of her poems in an anthology of young writers I co-edited in 2000, called *Oxygen*.[48] I knew her too as the author of a guide to the pubs of Wales,[49] and of a revealing first volume of poetry *Duwieslebog* ('Goddesslut'): "Picasso said that every woman / is either a goddess or a slut. / I am a goddesslut, / welcoming good and bad folk / into my life / filling buses with the nice ones / and falling in love with the misfits."[50] But we'd only met briefly before, when we both attended the 2005 Book of the Year awards evening in Cardiff, Elin as one of the three shortlisted authors for her first novel, and I as one of the longlisted ten for mine.

Elin's novel, *Rhwng Y Nefoedd a Las Vegas*[51] ('Between Heaven and Las Vegas'), is the story of a feisty young actress who gives up her career to marry a rough-diamond, jack-the-lad local boy, but who, in middle-age, finds herself hankering after an affair with an American professor with whom she'd had a college fling. Written from multiple viewpoints, it's witty, acerbic and unsparing in its impatience with the follies of its female characters. And if it's only slightly less impatient with the men, you get the impression that's only because less is expected of them. It's what reviewers call 'an impressive debut'.

The valley is stunningly beautiful: old mills, farmhouses, wild pheasants, straying ponies. As we drive through, Elin points out places of interest. The birthplace of the poet Ceiriog. The village halls. The place where the rock musician Roy Ward now lives. Ward joined the band City Boy as a drummer and vocalist in 1978 staying through the recording of their last three albums, and the big hit single '5-7-0-5' until they broke up in 1982. Twenty-five years later, fans still hail them as one of the great unsung bands of the seventies, and debate Ward's drumming and vocal skills on their website.⁵²

We pass the house where David Hunt, the Secretary of State for Wales between 1990 and 1993, used to live. As one of the string of four 'English' Welsh Secretaries during the days of the last Conservative government, he could at least claim some Welsh background, having spent his early childhood in Glyn Ceiriog. Thinking of him brought back a painful memory for me. In Elin's novel, the main character, the daughter of a Plaid Cymru politician, appears in the pages of *Wales on Sunday* after dancing topless on a nightclub table. Seeing David Hunt's house made me recall my own time with *Wales on Sunday*, as a young reporter, and my only conversation with Hunt himself.

At the time, there had been some controversy over how few of the Welsh rugby team could actually sing the national anthem. They'd been filmed before one international game chewing gum or staring into space instead of belting out the words of 'Hen Wlad fy Nhadau'. The news editor, thinking that this would be true of just about everyone in Wales, had the brilliant idea of running a picture gallery of famous Welsh people, none of whom could sing the anthem. Unfortunately, he knew how to make a good headline better than he knew how widespread the use of Welsh actually was.

"Call Max Boyce," he said. "He won't know it."

"Yes he will." I said. "He's a native Welsh speaker!"

"Is he?" he said, surprised. "Well phone Rhodri Morgan. Cardiff boy, Rhodri. He won't know it."

"But... he's a native Welsh speaker too. His father was a professor of Welsh."

"Really? Oh. Well phone Alun Michael. Cardiff South."

"He's a Welsh speaker too. He's from north Wales."

"Well, Paul Flynn, then, Newport West. No way he'll know it."

"He's *learned* Welsh."

But I couldn't find a convincing argument not to call David Hunt. So I had to, and I spoke to him at his home. He knew the anthem, of course, and was in the clear. In the end, the article had to run with a picture of some hapless HTV presenter who lived in Bristol and who wasn't even Welsh.

That, and dozens of humiliations like it, were the reasons I left *Wales on Sunday* after fifteen months, although it's ironic that, a few years later, the inability of David Hunt's successor, John Redwood, to sing the anthem at the Welsh Conservatives' conference caused a career-blighting furore. It's just as well no-one from *Wales on Sunday* had called him in advance with a query like mine, or he might have learned the words, and then the world would have been denied the sight of him goldfishing in the unforgiving glare of the cameras, a classic piece of video which Andrew Marr called "the most embarrassing political moment of all time."[53]

Elin and I had lunch in the Hand Hotel in Llanarmon Dyffryn Ceiriog. Appropriately, the pub has in its courtyard a wooden carving of a giant hand, sculpted from a local redwood tree by the artist Jim Heath. It's a reference to the 'Red Hand', the emblem of the Myddleton family, acquired, according to conflicting legends, either by the finding of a bloodstained handprint on a white tunic after a battle, or by the severing of the hand of one of two rival brothers settling a dispute through a race. The hotel is a sixteenth century farmhouse: real oak beams, real log fire, real ale, real chefs. The food is excellent. The ingredients are local. The waitress isn't. She's from Hungary. I try out my five words of Hungarian. *Igen. Nem. Jobb. Bal. Köszönöm.*[54] She brightens up.

Elin tells me about Glyn Ceiriog. Welsh is still strong here, certainly stronger than almost anywhere else in the Wrexham area. According to the 2001 census, forty-five per cent of the population of the valley could either speak, read, write or understand the language – nothing short of amazing considering the English border is minutes away. But, like everywhere, the language is beleaguered: locals moving out, outsiders moving in, and English pressing its way into vocabulary, grammar, syntax, homes, heads and hearts. Although, Elin says, things are rarely as simple as they appear; many incomers embrace the language, sending their children to learn it in the local school, which is, thanks to the efforts of campaigners, now Welsh-medium; some local Welsh speakers, meanwhile seem afflicted by an inferiority complex and can't seem to drop the language quickly enough, neglecting to pass it on to their children and opposing measures to promote it. While most of the rest of Wales has realised Welsh is now not merely a priceless piece of heritage but a valuable economic advantage, a few people here seem stuck in the last phases of an earlier cycle, in which the language was a sign of backwardness, something to be put aside with your hobnailed boots and your flat cap as you took the high road to England and advancement.

The road to England here is literally a high one. Coming in from eastwards over the ridge from Oswestry is the path taken in 1165 by the invading army of Henry II of England. He brought an army of thirty thousand men, many of them mercenaries, into Wales through

the Ceiriog Valley, intending to put an end to the independence of the powerful Welsh rulers Owain Gwynedd and Rhys of Deheubarth. As the invaders tried to clear a path through the ambush-filled forest, they cut down the oak trees as they went. But they spared one oak tree at Pontfadog, and it's still there, twelve hundred years old, and the oldest oak tree in Britain. A plaque put there to commemorate the golden jubilee of Henry's descendent, Elizabeth II, designates the oak as one of fifty 'Great British Trees'.

Oak trees were about the only victims of Henry's invasion. His enterprise failed ignominiously when his army met atrocious weather on the Berwyn mountains and retreated after a disastrous two weeks' campaign in which Welsh guerrilla tactics had caused the invaders heavy losses. Back in Shrewsbury, Henry revenged himself by having twenty Welsh hostages blinded. But that act of spite couldn't alter the fact that the combined forces of Gwynedd, Deheubarth and the Welsh weather had defeated him. No royal invasion was attempted for another fifty years; the battle in the Berwyns had bought Wales a precious half-century of freedom.

THE POETS' PANTHEON

The road Henry's army travelled is still called *Ffordd y Saeson*, 'The Road of the English'. On one slope alongside the road is a signboard depicting another, more recent, occasion in which Glyn Ceiriog was the scene of a battle between Wales and England. In 1923, Warrington Corporation wanted to acquire 13,600 acres of the valley and drown them to make a reservoir. Unlike the unluckier Capel Celyn forty years later, drowned by Liverpool Corporation despite all protests, this was one battle the natives managed to win. They were helped by the support of the former Prime Minister, David Lloyd George, who, calling the valley "a little bit of Heaven on earth", added his weight and his oratory to the protests. Warrington backed off.

Looking across the valley, with its alpine scenery and its string of idyllic-looking villages, it's easy to agree with Lloyd George's description, and it's easy to understand why the place has inspired so many authors. George Borrow made a special journey there, as he records in *Wild Wales*,[55] to visit the home of Huw Morys (1622-1709). Morys, known as *Eos Ceiriog*, 'The Nightingale of Ceiriog', was a gifted poet and an ardent Royalist at the time of the Civil War. He was a revered figure in his later life, and a memorial seat with the letters 'HMB' (for 'Huw Morys, Bard') was cut into the hillside near his home. It was this which Borrow wanted to see, and he dragged his guide, the householders and their servant through a wilderness of nettles, thorns and fallen branches in the pouring rain – "in a little time we were wet to the skin, and covered with the dirt of birds" – in order to find it. When he got there, he took off his hat and addressed his departed hero in Welsh:

'Shade of Huw Morys, supposing your shade haunts the place which you loved so well when alive — a Saxon, one of the seed of the Coiling Serpent, has come to this place to pay that respect to true genius, the *Dawn Duw*, which he is ever ready to pay. He read the songs of the Nightingale of Ceiriog in the most distant part of Lloegr, when he was a brown-haired boy, and now that he is a grey-haired man he is come to say in this place that they frequently made his eyes overflow with tears of rapture.'

I then sat down in the chair, and commenced repeating verses of Huw Morys. All which I did in the presence of the stout old lady, the short, buxom and bare-armed damsel, and of John Jones the Calvinistic weaver of Llangollen, all of whom listened patiently and approvingly, though the rain was pouring down upon them, and the branches of the trees and the tops of the tall nettles, agitated by the gusts from the mountain hollows, were beating in their faces, for enthusiasm is never scoffed at by the noble simple-minded, genuine Welsh, whatever treatment it may receive from the coarse-hearted, sensual, selfish Saxon.

Today Huw Morys is commemorated by a memorial located conveniently at the side of the main road through the valley. You can stop your car and pay homage with no danger of nettles or thorns. Or the dirt of birds. Borrow's own visit is commemorated with a plaque on the hillside behind the Ceiriog institute in Glyn Ceiriog itself. When I visited, Borrow's plaque was hidden behind an impenetrable barrier of branches from a fallen tree. It would have defied the most determined

literary pilgrim to get to it. I'm
sure Borrow would have appreciated the irony, noble, simple-
minded, genuine Saxon that he
was.

The Ceiriog Institute itself is
extraordinary. Outside, an unre-
markable village hall. Inside, a
jewel of stained glass and pol-
ished wood panelling. It was
built in 1911 to commemorate
the valley's most famous poet,
John Ceiriog Hughes (1832-
1887), known universally sim-
ply by his middle name, Ceiriog. He was a railway worker, a station-
master, but also a lyric poet of great simplicity and power. His poems of
love, loss and longing lent themselves readily to musical accompani-
ment, making him a hugely popular figure in his own time, and still
widely read and appreciated today. He was so popular that they built this
memorial hall to him, with all seven major Welsh banks of the day (their
crests of arms are commemorated in one of the windows) chipping in
to help with the cost.

If Welsh patriotism were a religion – and the two come very close in
some people's minds – then this is what its places of worship would look
like: small-scale, modest on the outside, but, for the chosen few on the
inside, a haven of lovingly-decorated familiar treasures, cherishing the
glories of the past, indifferent to the clamour of the present, and prizing
literature above above all other human endeavour. Ceiriog is there, an
Old Testament patriarch with bushy beard and no moustache. So is his
fellow poet Robert Ellis (Cynddelw) with even bushier beard, and,
again, no moustache. So is Huw Morys. Other windows commemorate
Mary Jones (1784-1872), the young girl from Llanfihangel-y-Pennant
who walked twenty-five miles barefoot to Bala to buy a Welsh Bible, and
Ann Griffiths (1776-1805), the young farmer's daughter from
Llanfihangel-yng-Ngwynfa, a few miles away in northern Powys, whose
poems expressed an ecstatic union with God such as only the rarest
mystics experience, and whose theology was so sophisticated that later
scholars marvelled how she could have conceived it. Underneath her
sunlit image, the text simply says 'Sweet Singer. Saint.'[56]

No engineers, statesmen, or explorers make it into the pantheon –
and certainly no soldiers. It's not that Welsh Wales hasn't produced

them, just that it doesn't value them like it values writers. Win a battle, govern a nation, devise an invention, cure a disease, and that's as may be. Fine if you like that kind of thing. But write a *poem*, now that's an achievement worth talking about. For that – at least if the poem's in Welsh and has won the National Eisteddfod – you'll be robed in purple, crowned and enthroned like a king. The risk-taking world-beater might be nodded to, politely, from a distance; but it's the harmless stay-at-home author who's embraced. As a value system, it's either completely loopy or deeply sane. I'm not sure which. But I know it means Wales is a very good place to be a poet.

A few hundred yards up the road from the institute is the former home of another author. Islwyn Ffowc Elis was born in Wrexham in 1924, and lived at Eirianfa, the house next to the chapel in Glyn Ceiriog, where he was brought up. He's best-known for his novel *Cysgod y Cryman* ('Shadow of the Sickle'), from 1953, and its 1956 sequel *Yn ôl i Lleifior* ('Return to Lleifior'). The first was the most popular Welsh-language novel of the twentieth century, and it went a long way towards establishing the novel as a widespread modern literary form in Welsh. It and its sequel were bestsellers; people queued to buy them, and even in 2007, three years after the author's death, the Welsh National Theatre was touring a successful stage show based on them. They tell the story of a Powys landowner's son whose Communist views conflict with his society's traditional values. Ground-breaking in their day, they're now painfully naive, although still uncannily readable.

The books made Elis a literary star, but the expectation of being a one-man industry producing agenda-setting popular books for his threatened culture was too much for him. He diverted his energies into radio work, politics, the church – in which he was ordained but soon resigned, disillusioned – and lecturing. Although none of his later work succeeded like his two bestsellers, he did produce *Wythnos yng Nghymru Fydd*, ('A Week in Future Wales'), a science fiction tale written in 1957, in which a time-traveller from 1950s Wales visits the

Wales of 2033, finding first an idyllic, independent, bilingual, pacifist paradise, but then, on a return visit, a nightmarish 'Western England' of endless forests, caravan parks, military ranges and reservoirs, in which the Welsh language has died. The moral is: the future can be changed, so decide now if it will be dream or nightmare. The book is naive, simplistic, and – in the scene where the time-traveller coaxes the words of the Twenty-third Psalm from the memory of the last surviving Welsh speaker – impossibly moving.

The Wales of 2033 is only twenty-six years away. But you only need to walk around Glyn Ceiriog to see that the Welsh-less dystopia envisioned in the novel will not become a reality by then, or anytime soon for that matter. We stopped at Theo Davies' workshop, where Elin's partner Peris works, just in time for the afternoon teabreak. The business which Theo Davies manages with his sons is at the other end of the wood-processing spectrum from Kronospan. Here, the wood isn't brought in by train, but selected from the local countryside, and hand-crafted into Welsh dressers, desks, bureaux, cabinets, even grandfather clocks. They're currently doing a brisk export trade in hand-made ash

walking frames for physiotherapy use. You name it, they can make it. They've been working here since 1946, and the workshop is a model of orderliness. Even the sawdust looked tidy. As we discussed the business, and the affairs of the village with Theo and his colleagues, Welsh was the only language heard. Apart from the voice of John Denver on the radio in the background, singing 'Country Roads'.

notes

1. A founder of the Social Democratic Party.
2. *No Truce With the Furies* (Bloodaxe, 1995).
3. Bridge Books, 2004, p18.
4. Later, Jacobitism became a catch-all title for anti-establishment campaigns, including political reform and Catholic emancipation.
5. Speaking, reading, writing and understanding, and all combinations of such abilities.
6. Pronounced "Ray-chee". Named after a friend's daughter, Rachel.
7. Meredith Edwards' son, Peter Edwards, became chair of the newly-formed Film Agency for Wales in 2006.
8. *The Independent*, 15 February 1999.
9. Williams *op. cit.*, p337.
10. She was also first runner-up in the Miss Universe competition that year.
11. When I last visited the market, the shop was gone.
12. *Dan Loriau Maelor*, (Gomer, 2003), p32.
13. I've tried to contact Wynne Lewis' daughter myself. Letters to the last known address, in Rödinghausen, are returned, *Empfänger nicht zu ermitteln*, addressee unknown. A phone call likewise, "*Leider*. No one of that name here" The internet yields nothing.
14. However, the area has still set the pace for choral music, with the Fron Choir, 'Britain's oldest boy band', enjoying an amazing run as a chart-topping classical album, and only narrowly missing out on a Classical Brit Award in 2007.
15. *Wild Wales*, Chapter 5.
16. An early fifteenth century wall-painting showing 'Works of Mercy', inscribed in Welsh, was found under later decorations in 1870.
17. The original house was built in the 1730s on an earlier Jacobean core. Destroyed by fire in 1858, it was replaced with the current building. A spectacular 1774 Snetzler organ moved to Wynnstay from the Williams-Wynns' London home in 1863 is now in the National Museum of Wales in Cardiff.
18. Moss Valley website: http://freepages.genealogy.rootsweb.com/~mossvalley/index.html
19. 'Fencible' regiments were for home defence only, unless all their members voted for overseas service. The Ancient Britons did so, putting down a rebellion in Ireland.
20. *Diaries of A Lady of Quality*, from 1797 to 1844, edited by A. Hayward, Esq, QC, Second Edition (Longman, Green, Longman, Roberts & Green) 1864.
21. www.nataliebennett.co.uk/
22. http://diariesofaladyofquality.blogspot.com/
23. The current, eleventh, baronet is, Sir David Watkin Williams-Wynn. His daughter Alexandra is believed to be the model for Lucien Freud's painting 'The Painter Surprised By A Naked Admirer'. Rowan Pelling, 'A woman of easel virtue', *The Independent*, 17 April 2005.
24. Kenrick (1848-1933) played five times for Wales, including once during Wales' first defeat of England, in 1881, as a last-minute substitute in his everyday clothes, Williams, *op.cit.*, p190.
25. Wrexham CBC: 'Story of Welsh Football': www.wrexham.gov.uk/english/heritage/welsh_football/1880_1914.htm
26. A double meaning: Meredith chewed a toothpick while playing. As he also chewed tobacco, the results were messy.
27. Winifred rarely watched her famous father play, as he didn't hold with women watching football. Brian Beard, 'Billy Meredith remembered,' http://womens.givemefootball.com/pfa14h.stm

28. It may date from the sixteenth century, but this can't be proved, as the school records were destroyed when Wynnstay Hall burned down in 1858.
29. *My Life and Loves*, 1924, p25.
30. James C. Simmons, 'Confessions of a Cowboy, An English Intellectual on a Texas Cattle Drive,' *The Austin Chronicle*, 26 May 2000.
31. Internet Movie Database: http://www.imdb.com/name/nm0364689/bio
32. Volume Four of his five-volume memoirs.
33. *Darluniau ar Gynfas*, (Gomer,1970)
34. Built between 1796 and 1801.
35. Built in 1846, but not by Telford. He died in 1834.
36. In 2005, local landowner John Pierce challenged Wrexham Council's right to charge him council tax, arguing his house formed part of the ancient Marcher lordship of Traian, one of 12 which escaped the 1535 Act of Union of England and Wales, and consequently tax-exempt. He paid up the day before a court hearing.
37. For more pictures, see 'R.S. Thomas, Priest and Poet', //members.aol.com/Nagaty2000/rst/ kept by Yoshifumi Nagata.
38. 'Chirk' may be an anglicised version of 'Ceiriog', the local river.
39. Medium-Density Fibreboard, High Density Fibreboard, Oriented Strand Board and Tongue and Groove.
40. The family keep a private apartment in the building.
41. The Myddletons have a place as patrons of Welsh culture, as one of them co-funded the first printing of the Welsh '*Beibl Bach*' the first handy-sized Bible, in 1630.
42. *Cydymaith i Lenyddiaeth Cymru*, (UWP 1997, p617.
43. Y Bywgraffiadur Arlein, National Library of Wales.
44. Heneage and Henry Ford in their biography of de Walden's set designer, Sidney Sime.
45. Rob Barnett, 'Joe Holbrooke – British Composer': http://www.musicweb-international.com/holbrooke/index.htm
    Michael Freeman, 'Joseph Holbrooke Incognito': http://www.musicweb-international.com/classrev/2003/Nov03/Holbrooke_Incognito.htm
    Michael Freeman, 'Joseph Holbrooke and Wales': http://www.musicweb-international.com/classrev/2003/Nov03/Holbrook_wales.htm
46. Named after David and Victoria Beckham's youngest boy, and actress Keira Knightley, whose names shot up the 'most popular' lists in 2005 and 2006. BBC: http://news.bbc.co.uk/1/hi/uk/6192247.stm
47. I lectured there in 2003 to an audience which included Mr David Owen, a direct descendent of Goronwy Owen.
48. Published by Seren and co-edited with Amy Wack.
49. *Tafarnau Cymru* (Y Lolfa, 1992).
50. *Oxygen* (Seren, 2000), p155.
51. Y Lolfa, 2004.
52. //cityboy.org/
53. //news.bbc.co.uk/1/hi/wales/3523872.stm The selection was made on the BBC's Politics Show. The second most embarrassing moment was Neil Kinnock falling into the sea at a party conference, and third was Prestatyn-born and Acrefair-educated John Prescott thumping a protestor at Rhyl. In the world of political embarrassment, Wales occupies the top three slots.
54. Yes. No. Right. Left. Thank you.
55. Chapter 20.
56. There's even one of the painted panels of St David used for the mosaics of the four nations of the United Kingdom in the lobby of the Houses of Parliament.

EAST

ENGLISH MAELOR

J.T. Vernon's Food Hall in Holt is doing a roaring trade. The customers are queueing out of the door, and are filling their reusable hessian carrier bags with the home-cured meats, the gluten-free sausages, the home-made ice cream and the farm preserves as fast as the straw-hatted staff can dish them out. This is a fourth-generation family firm which, starting as a horse-drawn farm butcher's business with a staff of one, is now a high-tech operation employing twenty-five and selling online. Outside, an antique bicycle with the company name commemorates the company's humble roots. New four-by-fours, twenty grand at least, draw up on the pavement; jumpered, tousel-haired thirtysomething dads climb out to collect their order of duck for the weekend, and to pick up the *Saturday Telegraph* from the corner shop. It's a colour supplement come to life. This is the kind of place where 'game' means pheasant not football.[1] I buy myself a pork pie, and take myself over to the bench on the village square to eat it. Fair play. It's the best I've ever tasted. And I never knew this shop existed. Even though I was brought up only about ten miles away, this is the first time I've been to Holt, the half-timbered town where a medieval stone bridge joins Wales to England across the river Dee. I take a look around me. Outside the Kenyon Hall, the metal-walled community centre, the Union Flag and the *Ddraig Goch* are flying side by side.

English Maelor. The name itself looks like a contradiction in terms. Maelor is a Welsh name, probably meaning a trading-floor, '*mael*' being an old word for trade or profit, and '*llawr*' meaning floor. That would make sense: this is a largely flat territory between the Welsh hills and the English plain. A place to meet and trade.

And to fight, of course. This exposed outlying area of Wales swung between Welsh and English control for centuries, eventually resulting in the Welsh foothills to the west being designated Maelor Gymraeg – Welsh Maelor – and the low lying eastern portion acquiring the title Maelor Saesneg, the English Maelor. The most famous conflict involving this district was in 616 AD, when the expansionist Anglian king of Northumbria, Aethelfrith, was looking to extend his power into the Anglo-Saxon kingdom of Mercia. For the Welsh in the kingdom of Powys on the western border of Mercia, neutrality wasn't an option. They'd learned to live with their new Anglo-Saxon neighbours, albeit uneasily. If they sat back and did nothing, and Mercia won, they could expect to suffer for their inaction. And Aethelfrith was an unknown quantity. Better the devil you know...

They joined forces with Mercia and met Aethelfrith's forces at Chester. To be on the safe side, the Welsh enlisted the help of 1200[2] monks from the monastery at Bangor-is-y-Coed (Bangor-on-Dee) to come with them and pray for victory. But their prayers went unheeded, and when Aethelfrith won, he had the monks massacred. Only fifty escaped. The Anglo-Saxon chronicler, the Venerable Bede, writing just over a century later,[3] had no sympathy. A mere thirteen years before the battle, Bangor's religious leaders had played a prominent role in a meeting between the native Celtic British church, which pre-dated the coming of the pagan Saxons, and St Augustine, representing the Roman Catholic church which had recently Christianised the invaders. The meeting was supposed to iron out differences, which, to Augustine's mind, meant the Celts submitting to Rome. They refused. So as far as Bede was concerned, the Bangor monks had backed the wrong side, theologically and politically, and massacre was all they deserved.

In the wake of the Battle of Chester, Bangor monastery, one of the greatest centres of learning in the Celtic world, was destroyed. Today, it's uncertain even exactly where it stood. The proxy location is the current parish church, itself vener-
able enough, with parts dating from as early as 1300. Its dedication - to St Dunawd, abbot of the former monastery – and its name, Bangor Monachorum, 'Bangor of the Monks,' keep the connection alive. Also keeping the connection alive is the animatronic monk which frightened the living daylights out of me as I wandered around the hushed interior one quiet weekday afternoon. As I passed its

alcove, I must have tripped some hidden switch and it creaked into life, raising its cowled head to look at me sightlessly.

The church stands on the banks of the river Dee, close to the five-arched seventeenth century stone bridge, attributed to Inigo Jones. For my visit to Maelor, I've enlisted the help of the doyen of Wrexham local historians, Derrick Pratt, who has an unrivalled knowledge of the area. He's keen on dispelling myths. He points out a road heading from Maelor in a straight three-mile trajectory to the hills to the west. "Just because it's straight, people think it must be Roman," he says. "But it's nothing of the sort. It's a coal road, built to bring coal from Rhos to the lowlands."

For my own part. I have few myths about the area to dispel. Maelor is undiscovered territory for me, so everything I learn is new. And I don't just learn about Maelor. Derrick Pratt points out that Wrexham itself has a castle. It was at Erddig, now better known for its beautifully-preserved stately home which is a National Trust property.[4] The castle, a wooden motte-and-bailey construction, seems to be medieval. Little remains of it, but it's probably the place referred to as 'Wristlesam' castle in official documents in 1161. Long overlooked and overgrown, there are now plans to clear the site and open it up for visitors, a record of the time when Wrexham was a potential battleground.

So much of the shape of this area dates from those times of border warfare. Even the administrative boundaries reflect past tensions. For centuries following the conquest, Maelor Saesneg was an administrative anomaly – part of Flintshire, but separated from the bulk of that county by a block of Denbighshire. Maelor Saesneg was known as 'Flintshire (Detached)', and shared that status with a scattering of other parish-sized enclaves, practising their different laws within surrounding Denbighshire, like Indian reservations. Most were consolidated with the larger county in 1885, but Maelor Saesneg and the smaller parish of Marford near Gresford retained their unique isolation until the wholesale local government reorganisation of 1974 when, as the last-surviving county enclaves in England and Wales, they became part of Clwyd. The later reorganisation of 1994 made them part of Wrexham.

OVERTON AND MARCHWIEL

When Daniel Defoe, author of *Robinson Crusoe*, visited Bangor in the 1720s, he tried to find the monastery, but without success: "as all the people spoke Welch, we could find no body that could give us any intelligence."[5]

Two and a half centuries later, it seems hard to believe that this area had been monoglot Welsh. The rolling countryside has an English feel. There's a full-sized white-railed racecourse at Bangor.[6] Welsh placenames are less frequent, and often diluted into anglicised forms. The settlement patterns are shire-like too. Not here the shoulder-to-shoulder solidarity of the industrial terraces of the hills. Instead, half-timbered houses, keeping a polite distance from one another, group themselves obediently around parish churches. Roads run straight and wide, a legacy of the enclosures of common land. Gentry houses guard their secrets behind tall gates and long drives.

Much of the settlement pattern dates from the English conquest of Wales in the late thirteenth century. The English knew it wasn't enough to defeat the Welsh in battle. You also had to keep the land you'd gained. And for that, you needed loyal settlers. They put together what today would be called a package of incentives to get the English to displace the Welsh natives. The low-lying districts of Maelor, new on the market, were a particularly attractive investment opportunity for the upwardly mobile Anglo-Saxon.

"There were people queueing up to come here," says Derrick Pratt. At Overton, the most important town in Maelor, he points out the characteristics which show that this town is an implanted one, dating from the time, in 1292, when it was granted a royal charter. From the start, it was laid out as an

English settlement, with orderly rectangular streets and plots of land ready to be handed out to the settlers willing to bring their wagon trains out to England's new wild western frontier. The territory gradually acquired the trappings of an English county: the sturdy, assertive castellated churches; the aloof, confident manor houses.

Pickhill Hall, near Marchwiel, is one of them.[7] In the late nineteenth century, the hall and its two hundred acre estate were bought by Harold Lees, son of a family of northern England factory-owners. He became a local squire and JP, but was killed in a hunting accident in 1887. He left the hall, and his fortune, to his nephew, Gilbert,[8] an action which gave Wrexham a footnote in the history of one of the English-speaking world's greatest poets – because Gilbert's daughter, Georgie Hyde-Lees, married William Butler Yeats.

Although he spent most of his life in London's clubland, Gilbert Hyde-Lees gave Pickhill Hall as his address, presumably because it suited his image to have a country seat. When Georgie married Yeats on 20 October 1917. The *Irish Times* announcement read: "Yeats and Hyde-Lees – Oct 20, 1917. In London, W.B. Yeats, to Georgie, only daughter of the late W.G. Hyde-Lees, of Pick Hill Hall, Wrexham, and of Mrs Henry Tucker, of 16, Montpellier Road, London."[9] Georgie had been born in London in 1892, and there seems no evidence of her ever having lived at Pickhill Hall, although biographies of Yeats and articles often show her as being 'of Wrexham'. Her parents separated, and she spent most of her youth in the south of England.[10]

She married Yeats when he was fifty-two and she was only twenty-five. They were fellow members of the Hermetic Order of the Golden Dawn, an occult group. When they met, Yeats was privately working to a self-imposed deadline to get married and father a child to carry on the family name. He'd recently proposed for the fourth time (or fifth depending on your source) to the love of his life, the charismatic Irish nationalist Maud Gonne. When she rejected him yet again, he proposed to Maud's daughter, Iseult. And when she rejected him too, he turned to Georgie, and proposed to her.

They were a week into their honeymoon when she found out that he'd married on the rebound, and was still writing to Iseult. Georgie's response was original. Only hours after getting the news, she began to experience a phenomenon called automatic writing, in which she would compose while apparently under the direction of the spirit world. In her book *Yeats' Ghosts: The Secret Life of W.B. Yeats*, the biographer Brenda Maddox points out that Georgie's initial writings bore a striking resemblance to the contents of Marie Stopes' *Married Love*, a relationship guide which stressed the husband's duty to satisfy his wife sexually. Yeats would sit with Georgie for hours, questioning the spirits, and painstakingly recording their replies.

Whether genuine or not, the automatic writing saved the marriage. Georgie bore Yeats a daughter in 1919 and a son in 1921. Georgie also professed to be a medium, and frequently took part in *séances* with Yeats and his circle. Their occult interests lasted their lifetimes. Yeats himself died in 1939, and Georgie survived him by twenty-nine years, dying on 23 August 1968, aged seventy-seven. She lies beside him in Drumcliff churchyard near his childhood home in County Sligo.

She isn't the only famous medium with a Wrexham connection. Living TV's Derek Acorah, star of the *Most Haunted* series, once played for Wrexham FC, in a football career that took him to Liverpool, Stockport County, Glentoran and Australia. As a footballer, and one-time protégé of the legendary Bill Shankly, he was known as Derek Johnson, but he changed his second name to Acorah when he began his second, and more successful, career as a TV medium. *Most Haunted* specialises in visits to depressing, empty sites with an atmosphere of impending doom. Not too different to playing for Wrexham, really.

HANMER

Before it was bought by Georgie Hyde-Lees' family, Pickhill Hall had been the home of the Puleston family, Norman carpetbaggers come to enjoy the spoils of Edward I's conquest in 1282. One of them, Roger de Pyvelisdon, was made Sheriff of Anglesey, but was lynched by a Welsh mob in 1304 when he tried to collect English taxes, an imposition to which, *Burke's Peerage* mildly puts it, the Welsh were 'averse'. A century later, the Pulestons had gone native, intermarried with Welsh nobility, had thrown themselves into Owain Glyndŵr's glorious, but ultimately doomed, War of Independence,[11] and were patrons of Welsh poets such as Guto'r Glyn, Gutun Owain and Lewys Glyn Cothi.

In the history of Glyndŵr's fight for freedom, 'English' Maelor has a major role. Owain himself was born in 1359, of princely Welsh descent, and when his father died, it's believed he was fostered out, aged about eleven, to an Anglo-Welsh judge called Sir David Hanmer, living at the settlement of the same name in Maelor. From him, Glyndŵr acquired both the profession of law, and a wife, Sir David's daughter, Margaret, whom Glyndŵr married in St Chad's church in Hanmer in 1383.[12] Seventeen years later, in 1400, the Hanmer family

were drawn into the conflict when a border dispute between Glyndŵr and a high-handed Norman neighbour in Ruthin escalated into a full-scale war of independence, a war which produced Wales' first taste of political freedom since the Edwardian conquest in 1282, and its last until a measure of self-government was restored with the opening of the National Assembly in 1999.

St Chad's is a towering structure on the top of a hill. Inside, near the altar, a plaque, and a coat of arms in Owain Glyndŵr's distinctive red and gold colours mark the spot where the Welsh prince-to-be and his English bride were married. It was a match typical of the co-existence of the border nobility of the time. As they joined hands that day, neither could have guessed that less than two decades later, they would be at the centre of a war that would lay an entire country waste, that would leave the bride a prisoner in the Tower of London, and that would leave the groom a never-to-be-captured fugitive.

The defeat of Glyndŵr's rebellion meant the end of hopes of Welsh political independence, but it had little effect on the strength of Welsh culture, which continued as creatively as before. In fact, freed from the necessity of constant warfare, the Welsh nobility now had more time to devote to the arts. One such was Dafydd ab Edmwnd, one of the Hanmer family, who had lands in the village and who is reputed to be buried in Hanmer church. He was born somewhere around the end of Glyndŵr's princedom, and became one of the greatest of the Welsh poets of the nobility. He was at the height of his powers in the late fifteenth century and his use of the twenty-four metres of traditional Welsh poetry became the basis for the rules which governed the artform for centuries. His was the last word on matters of form. But he was no mean stylist either. His 'Cywydd Merch', addressed to a girl, concludes "Dy garu di a gerais / dy gas im nis dygai Sais," "I have loved loving you: / no Englishman would hate me so."

As you emerge into the sunlight and look down across the well-kept graveyard, you are faced with the gleaming expanse of Hanmer mere, one of the network of post-glacial lakes which stud this area of

Wales and Shropshire. Everything looks as serene as a country village is supposed to be.

But the mere contains cold, dark, dangerous currents. And so does village life, even for a child of the local vicarage – at least if you believe the autobiography of one of Hanmer's children, Lorna Sage. Her life-story, *Bad Blood*,[13] was published in 2000. Previously, Sage, a talented, independent-minded professor at the University of East Anglia, had produced only academic books, albeit impressive ones. She was regarded as one of the most acute literary critics of her generation. *Bad Blood*, though, was something else. It was a memoir of her childhood as the grand-daughter of the vicar of Hanmer, and of her adolescence at Whitchurch in Shropshire. But no ordinary memoir. *The Times*[14] spoke of its "spellbinding, jawdropping frankness", *The Guardian* called it "almost unbearably eloquent". Critics throughout the English-speaking world queued up to praise it. It was partly the effortless, laconic style, but also the unsparing candour with which she describes the physical, emotional and spiritual grubbiness of life in an austerity-hit, post-war backwater which seemed almost a nineteenth century enclave, and which was the hated place of exile of as dysfunctional a family as you could ever fear to meet. The opening paragraphs give the idea:

> Grandfather's skirts would flap in the wind along the churchyard path and I would hang on. He often found things to do in the vestry, excuses for getting out of the vicarage (kicking the swollen door, cursing) and so long as he took me he couldn't get up to much. I was a sort of hobble, he was my minder and I was his. He'd have liked to get further away, but petrol was rationed. The church was at least safe. My grandmother never went near it – except feet first in her coffin, but that was years later, when she was buried in the same grave with him.
>
> Rotting together for eternity, one flesh at the last after a lifetime's mutual loathing. In life, though, she never invaded his patch; once inside the churchyard gate he was on his own ground, in his element. He was good at funerals, being gaunt and lined and marked with mortality. He had a scar down his hollow cheek, too, which Grandma had done with the carving knife one of the many times when he came home pissed and incapable.

You couldn't accuse Sage of looking at the world through rose-coloured glasses. The spectacular failings of her family and the wider society are laid bare in a style whose unsensational matter-of-factness simply makes the story all the more hypnotising: blackmail, adultery, booze, rage, hatred and deceit. And those were the good days. Books were her refuge. She sought sanctuary in endless reading, a process which led, despite an accidental pregnancy at sixteen, to an against-the-odds academic career, and escape.

She was in her late fifties when she wrote her cathartic, ghost-laying retrospective. It became a number one bestseller, winning the Whitbread Prize for Biography. But Sage had only a week to enjoy her success. Plagued for years by emphysema, on 11 January 2001, she died.

While Sage's portrait of Hanmer is of merciless, unremitting squalor, many locals remember the place, and the characters, differently. In the church you can pick up a leaflet which says Lorna's grandfather, Canon Meredith Morris, is remembered "with respect and affection" by people in Hanmer, and that his preaching, pantomimes and shows drew people in from far and wide. It contains the memories of some of Sage's contemporaries, who have their own version of the events in the book. Sportingly, however, the leaflet offers a 'Bad Blood Trail' around the village in which visitors can view the locations of Sage's adventures "in an easy ten minute stroll".

TALLARN GREEN

Lorna Sage's world of teenage mothers, boozy philandering priests and intolerant prying neighbours seems to belong in a different age, and to somewhere less genteel than Maelor Saesneg seems to be today. But there is one part of the district where a woman who had a child out of wedlock would have been at home, and wouldn't have had to worry about what the neighbours might say.

The place is called Threapwood, a parish on the border with Maelor Saesneg, but partly in Cheshire, and therefore, in the past, technically an 'extra-parochial' no-man's land between the respective parishes. In the days when parishes were the only form of local government and law-enforcement, this status mattered. It meant Threapwood was exempt from all local laws. Crucially, this meant any child born there had no claim on parish assistance if they were in poverty. So neighbouring parishes used it as a dumping ground for any pregnant girl who looked likely to be a burden on the rates. Or as John Jones put it more delicately in 1859 in *Wrexham and its Neighbourhood*:

> ...from time immemorial a place of refuge for the frail fair, who made here a transient abode clandestinely to be freed from the consequences

of illicit love... For this reason the churchwardens and overseers drove a busy trade in exporting thither all the frail fair to secure Threapwood as the birthplace of all those who "came saucily into the world somewhat before they were sent for".

Cast adrift from society, and freed from social constraints, Threapwood, in response, valued its freedom as a refuge for outlaws. S. Lewis, in *A Topographical Dictionary of Wales* in 1834, described it as "long the resort of abandoned characters of every description, and especially of women of loose or blemished morals... The inhabitants, considering themselves beyond the reach of all legal authority, opposed, even with force, the execution of the assize and other laws within their precinct."

Derrick Pratt agrees: "This was debatable land. Serving wenches in the family way, deserters from the army, vagrants. They met here and shacked up together in their own cottages. The area became such a problem, with questions asked in the House of Commons about the state of wantonness there, that they decided that a church had to be built there. It was only really sorted out in 1894 when some new counties came into being."

Control of the area was tugged back and fore between the counties of Cheshire and Flintshire, and between the dioceses of Chester and St Asaph, for a century and more until it was finally made part of Chester diocese in 1920, at the disestablishment of the Church in Wales, when border parishes were being parcelled out between Wales and England like property in a divorce settlement.[15] That divorce finally made an honest parish out of Threapwood.

A short distance away from Threapwood, in a little valley in the very easternmost part of Wales, is a church whose history is a legacy of that period when Welsh and English Anglicans went their separate ways. St Mary's Church, Whitewell, is a brick-built and white-painted early nineteenth century building on the site of a much earlier church. Just how early can be guessed from the fact that there are two holy

wells here, a sure sign of ancient sanctity. But it's uniqueness comes
from more recent times. This is the only church in north Wales still
part of the Church of England. When, in 1920, the Anglican Church
in Wales was being stripped of its status as state religion and made
into a separate province, many border parishes wanted to stay in the
CofE, and so with the status quo. But only a handful in Radnorshire
and Monmouth-shire succeeded, and in north Wales, just this one.

The church contains a memorial to one of Wrexham's two winners
of the Victoria Cross in World War Two,[16] Captain Bernard Armitage
Warburton-Lee, killed on 10 April 1940, when leading a destroyer
flotilla against a superior force of German warships at Narvik in
Norway.[17]

The same year that Captain Warburton-Lee died in action, the
nearby parish of Tallarn Green got a new priest, one who took a very
different view of warfare. As mentioned earlier, the young R.S.
Thomas had had to move from Chirk because he'd got married, and
his vicar didn't want a married curate. It was at Tallarn Green,[18]
which overlooks Threapwood from the Welsh side of the border, that
this refined young man found refuge – probably the only person ever
sent there for the sin of being married.

Thomas was stationed at Tallarn Green until 1942. He was a pacifist, never an easy or a popular position to adopt during wartime.
Now aged twenty-seven, the sensitive young curate was troubled by
the sin and destructiveness exemplified by the nightly bombing raids
he could see taking place on Liverpool. One night in late August, he
was watching the raid which set the mountain near Minera on fire,
and which was mentioned earlier in the section on the Clywedog
Valley. As he watched, he came to a singular response, one which
would have a profound effect on later Welsh literary history. He
decided he was going to learn Welsh.

It's not the most obvious reaction to a bombing raid. But it made
sense to Thomas at the time. He idealised rural pre-industrial life.
And what he saw in the fires above Minera wasn't good against
evil, or fascism against freedom – it was industrialism versus the
human spirit. He saw fleets of aeroplanes from one giant industrial
power delivering hundreds of tons of high explosive onto the cities
and factories of another great industrial power hundreds of miles
away. Mass-produced modernity leading to madness and mayhem.
The answer, he believed, was to return to a more innocent age,
before aeroplanes, before factories, before petrol engines, before
trains, before towns even. And, crucially, to a time before the

English language had polluted what he believed was a pristine idyll of Welsh folk life. Learning Welsh would be his way of challenging 'The Machine' as his later poems came to call the complex inter-action of industry, science and society in the modern world.

The rest of his life was a journey in response to that impulse. He moved west – to his first job as vicar – in Manafon in Montgomeryshire in 1942, a place where tractors and electricity hadn't yet penetrated. Then, in 1954, he went further west still, to Eglwysbach near Machynlleth, and then, in 1967, as far west as it's possible to go – to Aberdaron at the tip of the Llŷn peninsula. Getting more westerly and more Welsh every time. Towards the end of his life, Thomas was widely recognised as being, with Dylan Thomas, one of the two great Welsh poets of the twentieth century. He was even nominated for a Nobel Prize. It would have been fitting if that award, established by a con-science-stricken explosives manufacturer, should have gone to a man whose poetic career was sparked by watching ton after ton of high explosive set a Welsh mountain on fire.

I did my doctoral thesis on R.S. Thomas, and knew him quite well. I once spent a morning with him at his cottage in Rhiw on the Llŷn peninsula, fifty years after he had made his flight westwards. And I spent years with his poems, in which empty rural churches, cold chancels, bare altars and draughty naves serve as metaphors for the harsh material world in which man searches for a tantalisingly-absent God. So I can never visit a deserted rural church without feeling as though I'm enacting one of Thomas' poems. That feeling accompanies me as I open the door to St Mary's.

The Victorian church, opened in 1873, is a little jewel of a place, with a steep pitched roof, an apsidal end and a delicate clock tower. Appropriately enough, the building is dedicated to St Mary Magdalene; perhaps the church fathers thought the story of the repentant sinful woman would be a useful example to the dissolute neighbours on the ungodly east side of the river.

Inside, the place is spotless, homely rather than austere, and lovingly-maintained, with rich stained glass and some tasteful, glossy information boards giving the history of its most famous former priest. Somehow, the place looks too fresh, too new to have been the church of a man who died in 2000 in his late eighties. But churches have different life cycles to mortals. In ecclesiastical terms, this is still a young building.

I try to imagine R.S. Thomas here. Younger then than I am now, he would have stalked to this very pulpit to look out over his parish-ioners. From his lofty position, he would have seen, staring back at him from the far end of the church, a bold stained-glass St Michael, in suit of armour, iron foot on the neck of the Serpent, sword in hand. Pacifist priest and warrior archangel facing one another above the congregation's heads. The priest has long gone into the west, seeking his elusive sanctuary. St Michael still stares out, unblinking.

CROESO, WELCOME, WITAMY

The tides of war created one of Wrexham's most distinctive communities – the Poles. At the end of the war, a Polish mobile military medical centre, a kind of MASH unit with vodka, located in the village of Penley in English Maelor after spending the war treating Polish and Allied combatants in places as diverse as Africa, Italy, Persia, Palestine and Iraq, part of the army of around 250,000 Polish expatriates displaced by the conflict.[19]

When the war ended, the Poles had the choice of returning home. But with the Soviet Union now in control there, the vast majority chose to stay in the west. They wanted to stay together, and they needed a hospital for their war veterans and their families. Penley, a former US army hospital and later a centre for denazification of German prisoners, was chosen because it had hospital facilities and was conveniently close to Liverpool, the port to which the Polish Army had been shipped at the end of hostilities.

At its height, the Penley complex housed two thousand Polish staff and patients, had its own cinema, theatre, shop, canteen and club and was a centre for Polish patients from all over Britain.

They had their own chapel – now demolished – kept their own festivals, when children in national costume would parade round the district, and created their own religious art. For a time, the Royal Oak pub in Wrexham High Street was nicknamed 'The Polish Embassy', as there were so many exiled Poles among its clientele. The nickname long survived the war period, and in the 1980s the pub was briefly renamed 'The Embassy' in belated com-memoration.[20]

The Poles left their mark in many ways: Wrexham's Catholic Cathedral holds a monthly Polish mass; Wrexham Cemetery in Ruabon Road has a memorial to the many Polish military personnel who are buried there; Penley's quaint thatched local primary school, Madras Voluntary Aided,[21] greets website visitors with

'Croeso, Welcome, Witamy'. Polish surnames are common locally: the most famous instance probably being Eddie Niedzwiecki, the Wrexham, Chelsea and Wales goalkeeper, and television football commentator. Although born in Bangor, he joined Wrexham as a schoolboy at fourteen, and was in the promotion-winning Wrexham squad in 1978.

For many years, the *Wrexham Leader* would carry occasional adverts seeking Polish-speaking medical staff for Penley. But over time, the adverts' requirements changed as the population aged, assimilated and dispersed: requests for gynaecologists or paediatricians became requests for specialists in geriatric medicine. Today, a small modern unit still serves the ageing residents. Its sign is in English, Welsh and Polish

Many of the buildings survive, unmistakeably standard army-issue single-storey blocks. Some are factories, workshops, offices. Some are decaying. At the church in Penley is one of the most poignant locations: the unmarked grave of sixty-seven Polish babies, born in the immediate post-war period to parents so undernourished and weakened by war that their children lacked the strength to survive. Derrick Pratt tells me they had a life-expectancy of between eighteen hours and six weeks. Their parents, and many other Poles lie here too, their headstones in orderly ranks, the epitaphs in Polish. On All Saints' Day, relatives place jam jars with candles on the graves.

The irony, though, is that there are now more Poles in Wrexham than were ever here during the war. Eight thousand at the last count; some say ten thousand. Nearly seven per cent of the population, and around three per cent of the quarter of a million Poles who migrated

to the UK after Poland entered the EU in 2004. As Wrexham accounts for only 0.22 per cent of the UK population, that makes the town, proportionately, one of the most Polish in Britain. If London had a similar proportion of Poles, it would have nearly half a million. Along with neighbouring Flintshire, Wrexham has a quarter of all the Polish migrants to Wales. Not bad for counties which, together, count for less than six per cent of the Welsh population. Cardiff might have the Assembly, the Millennium Stadium, and the Wales Millennium Centre, but as far as the Poles are concerned, it can't compete with Wrexham, the Welsh Warsaw.

The fact that Wrexham had a long-standing Polish community was crucial in attracting this second wave of migrants. It's hard to know to what degree there is awareness of Wales in Poland, although the Polish Pope John Paul II did visit Wales in 1982 and managed a couple of phrases of Welsh. There's one part of Poland, however, where knowledge of the Welsh language is a little more widespread. In the historic city of Lublin, the Catholic University actually has a department which teaches Welsh.[22] This was the only Catholic institution of higher education in the old Soviet empire. Before he became pope, the Rev. Karol Wojtyla□a held the Chair of Ethics in the Department of Christian Philosophy here. Such religion as survived elsewhere in the communist bloc was mainly Eastern Orthodox, and eastward-looking. But the Poles, as Catholics, looked west, and Catholicism was therefore seen as a potentially subversive element by the Soviet authorities.[23] As a policy of quiet, academic subversion, the university fostered a western world view, including the study of American and British culture. Amazingly, the British section included study of both Irish and Welsh. Irish, at a Catholic University, I could just about understand. But Welsh? That Catholic convert Saunders Lewis, founder of Plaid Cymru, would have thought it a dream come true.

I visited there as a lecturer at a festival of British culture in 2003, and was amazed to find students and former students who could converse, to varying degrees, in the language of heaven thanks to the teaching programme which was, by then, well into its second decade. I wondered if this was the reason why so many of them – many more than I had expected, had turned up for my talk. I was lecturing on the history of the relationship between the Welsh and Jewish people. I found out, as the packed lecture hall emptied after the event, that most of them had come by mistake, believing me to be the distinguished Polish-speaking British historian Sir *Norman* Davies, author of the magisterial history of Poland, *God's Playground*, who was also taking part in the festival. I can only hope they weren't too disappointed.

Nearly all the Wrexham Poles are now young adults. A public order problem? Not necessarily, but just in case, PC Keith Sinclair learned Polish in order to make better contacts with them.[24] North Wales Police chief constable, Richard Brunstrom even mooted the idea of recruiting Polish-speaking officers. The *Daily Express* lined up Tory politicians to condemn him, citing his previous convictions for controversy, including being made an honorary druid by the Gorsedd of Bards for learning Welsh – just about permissible for a native Welshman, but deeply suspicious behaviour for an Englishman. Dangerous business, learning other languages. Must be something wrong with the fella. Gone native. Can't be trusted.

The first migrants were men coming alone, many sending money back to families in Poland. Soon, families came too, and in eighteen months, the number of children in Wrexham schools with English as a foreign language jumped from three hundred to five hundred, and in one year Wrexham's Victoria Junior School saw the proportion of its children with English as a second language grow from five per

cent to eleven per cent. 'A challenge', the council says. But one it's dealing with. Victoria's head teacher, John Hughes, has recruited specialist teachers, including one Pole, to help integration.[25]

Not everyone in Wrexham is as sanguine. Newspaper letters pages contain complaints about the Poles' and others' impact on jobs, housing, social services. Those are the ones fit to print. Message boards and

blogs seethe with unmoderated, misspelt resentment: wages being undercut, benefits being scrounged, they say. There are counter-arguments, of course: the Poles are workers; they pay taxes; they earn money and spend it locally; they're young, dynamic, reliable and industrious. But the fears are fertile ground for right-wing political groups like the BNP, who polled nearly ten per cent of the regional vote in Wrexham during the May 2007 National Assembly elections, contributing to a total tally in north Wales which brought them within a couple of thousand votes of a regional list seat.

When, just under twenty years ago, I came across evidence of far-right recruitment in Wales in my work as a journalist, I found it hard to believe. Even harder to believe was that the campaigners were avoiding the boots-and-flags skinhead brutalism of the 1970s National Front, and were, instead appealing to the kind of green-tinged, folksy, back-to-the-land, blood-and-soil idealism which had inspired some of the earliest twentieth century fascists in the days before their followers traded their home-made clogs for jackboots and tried to take over the world. The new campaigners' literature expressed sympathy for Welsh culture and quoted Saunders Lewis approvingly. Intriguing, I thought, but surely a sign of desperation. This mutation of British fascism would surely not live long. But when a figure on the fringes of the British security services tipped me off that Nick Griffin, a former senior NF member, had moved to Wales, I had to investigate further.

It took me days to find him. The address I'd been given led me on a false trail in rural Gwent. But then I managed to find the remote cottage in the hills near Cefn Einion on the Shropshire border, where far-right sympathisers had been rumoured to be holding gatherings. I staked it out for days from the hillside opposite, watching with binoculars for movements, and carrying a mobile telephone which had been given to me to call for back-up. The phone wasn't quite the size of a housebrick. It was quite a bit bigger. And heavier. This was 1993, and mobile phones looked like the kind of thing a World War Two radio operator would carry. What's more, in this remote border area its signal wouldn't work. You had to drive fifty miles in the direction of the nearest big town to get reception. It would have to be a very slow-moving emergency if this bit of kit was to be of any use.

The hideout was at the bottom of an isolated valley, invisible from any other dwelling. Eventually, I satisfied myself there was no-one there, and made my way down the track towards it. I reasoned if anyone came out and went for me, I'd have a head start, aided by fear, and could outrun them. If I ditched the phone, of course. Then I wondered – what if they had a dog? One of those vicious pitbulls that skinheads seem to like so much, one that would come for me like a fanged white exocet, phone or no phone. Mind you, maybe I could throw the phone at it.

The farm was deserted. Thankfully. I looked in through the windows. There was one of those Arts Council of Wales posters with an early Welsh poem 'Eryr Pengwern'. Cultured skinheads? Had I got the wrong place? I walked up the steps of one of the outbuildings and pushed open the door to the first-floor chamber. No, this was the place all right: there was a printing workshop with piles of far-right leaflets, teeshirts and designs. One showed a hand giving a Nazi salute, another showed a blood-dripping knife and the words 'Rivers of Blood', a reference to the notorious anti-immigration speech by Enoch Powell.[26] I photographed them all for the record.

But I still hadn't got proof of a connection with Griffin. There was one way to find out. I went through the house's black waste bag looking for discarded correspondence. I found it, in the form of a letter written to the house's new tenant by Griffin, from his new address near Welshpool. I left the farm, drove to Welshpool, and found the house, a big leafy respectable-looking rectory-style property. I knocked. The householder told me Griffin had lived there but had moved on. They had a forwarding address, however, in Llanerfyl, a few miles away.

I went to that property, a remote hilltop cottage, with a camera crew. We'd only get one chance to get the pictures. Griffin was there, initially surprised at being doorstepped, but recovering in a moment, and with an answer for everything. I got the impression he rather enjoyed it. Any publicity... He was cool, plausible, and articulate. Afterwards, I found out that since moving there, he'd been active in the campaign to save the local primary school. No-one knew his background. We found footage of him at a demonstration, holding a protest banner. Holding the other end was an officer of the local anti-apartheid group, blissfully unaware he was standing shoulder-to-shoulder with Britain's leading right-wing demagogue.

At the time, much as it made a good programme, I considered the whole matter a curiosity rather than anything of lasting significance. Surely this lot would never attract more than a few cranks, would be easily contained and would soon split apart under the fractiousness that afflicts all such fringe groups. In a series of articles at the time, I ventured to predict accordingly. But nearly twenty years on, they had a party structure, widespread publicity, and one in ten of the voters in my own home town were backing them.

It's still a blip, I feel sure of it. But all the same I don't think I'll venture any firm predictions on what will happen. Experience teaches caution. Twenty years ago, I would never have predicted the advent of a group who would combine the seemingly irreconcilable elements of British and Welsh nationalism, and I certainly didn't foresee that such a strange cocktail would appeal to even as many as one in ten of the electorate in a Welsh Assembly election. But then, at that time, who would have predicted there would be such a thing as a Welsh Assembly? And even ten years ago, who would have predicted Wrexham would be home to ten thousand Poles? All the same, I hope the hostility is short-lived. For sixty years and more Wrexham people have known the benefit Polish people have brought, and have been proud of it, even as the Poles have been proud of their Welsh home. The future can be a very strange country indeed, but whatever that country's like, I hope it's one where mutual pride has proved stronger than the fear.

notes

1. Although the area does have some footballing connections, as the birthplace of legendary Welsh international goalkeeper Leigh Richmond Roose, (1877 1916), killed at the Somme. Roose's brother Edward earned a footnote in literary history when , in 1887, and a pupil at Holt Academy, 'an impoverished boarding school', he kicked one of his teachers, H.G. Wells (then aged 21 and later to become the pioneering science-fiction novelist) so badly that he suffered a crushed kidney and lung haemorrhages, and had to leave the school.
2. An impossible number, of course. Theories abound as to how many there actually could have been.
3. In *A History of the English Church and People*.
4. And notable for the unusual care which its former owners, the Yorkes, took to record the lives of their servants, whose likenesses they preserved in formal portraits.
5. *Tour Through the Whole Island of Great Britain*, letter VII.
6. A racecourse since 1859, and the only one in the UK without a grandstand. Instead, the site makes use of a natural amphitheatre shape to allow spectators to watch the proceedings.
7. At the time of writing, the lodge to Pickhill Hall, described as 'simply charming', was for sale at £405,000.
8. From Ann Saddlemyer, *Becoming George, The Life of Mrs W.B. Yeats*, (OUP, 2002), p14.
9. *Ibid*, p100.
10. Gilbert Hyde-Lees died of drink and syphilis in a home for alcoholics in 1909.
11. The Pulestons' original seat in the area was Emral Hall, now demolished. They moved to Pickhill Hall later. They have a memorial in the meticulously-preserved church at Worthenbury near Overton.
12. Owain Glyndŵr:

http://www.bbc.co.uk/wales/history/sites/owain_glyndwr/pages/background.shtml
13. Fourth Estate.
14. 27 September 2000.
15. It became a separate parish in 1968.
16. The other is Flight Lieutenant David Lord, born in 1913, and educated at St Mary's Roman Catholic School in Wrexham, who was killed in September 1944 piloting a Dakota aircraft at Arnhem.
17. He is buried at Narvik. Williams, *op.cit.*, p315.
18. The village is also notable for having visible remnants of a medieval field system, and, like Penley, a Madras school. See 'Croeso, Welcome, Witamy,' p176.
19. Polish WW2 Forces: http://felsztyn.tripod.com/id12.html
20. The pub reverted to its original name before being changed again to 'Via Alto', and, following the new Polish influx, it is once again 'The Embassy'.
21. The school was founded in 1811 by the Second Lord Kenyon, the first free school in Wales, on education principles pioneered by Dr Andrew Bell, a Scottish clergyman who developed his ideas in Madras, India.
22. Catholic University of Lublin: http://www.kul.lublin.pl/uk/
23. They were right; in 1980 most of the university's workers and students joined the Solidarity protest
24. PC Keith Sinclair:
http://www.bbc.co.uk/wales/northeast/guides/halloffame/public_life/keith_sinclair.shtml
PC Plodski: http://uk.news.yahoo.com/21112006/144/pc-plodski.html
There was a bit of a problem for the council though, which introduced a 100-question test to make sure Polish would-be taxi-drivers actually had 'The Knowledge'.
25. 'Can schools manage migrants?' http://news.bbc.co.uk/1/hi/uk/5388264.stm
26. Whose family were from Wrexham. On one side, his family were the Breeses, who ran printing businesses in the town, and who counted a mayor of Wrexham, Ethel Claire Breese, among their number. Powell himself learned Welsh and once gave a television interview in the language.

PARALLEL
WREXHAMS

I must have been particularly homesick that day. A student visiting London, I was waiting at a train station, and, in the absence of any other reading material, was flicking through the A-Z. So many streets. So many different names employed to personalise the maze of the capital's streets, names ranging from the exotic to the stunningly mundane: an empire of countries; a complete collection of poets; lectionaries of saints; pantheons of heroes; directories of surnames and dynasties of monarchs. And what appeared to be a close-to-comprehensive gazetteer of towns. Towns. I looked through the W's. Yes, there it was: Wrexham Road. It wasn't very long. It wasn't very central. But it was there, and suddenly, I didn't feel quite so far from home.

More than twenty years later, during a visit to London, I cut myself a free afternoon and took the tube to Bow, the nearest station to Wrexham Road. This neighbourhood, part of Tower Hamlets, is traditionally popular with immigrants; London's East End equivalent of the Lower East Side, attracting successive communities of Jewish and Irish incomers, each of whom, as their prosperity increased and they moved out, made way for a succeeding wave. Now, the area is the heartland of London's Bangladeshi community. I checked my A-Z and set off in the general direction, somewhat apprehensively, not knowing whether the area might be hostile to the appearance of a man with a camera. I remember filming on the street in Brixton in the early nineties; I and the cameraman were simply getting some establishing shots of the neighbourhood, but were subjected to a seemingly unbroken stream of drive-by, and walk-by verbal abuse, triggered by the sight of a film camera in an area where suspicion of outsiders was high. There are areas where it's safer to produce a gun than a camera. I hoped this wasn't one of them.

Certainly, the hoodie count in Bow seemed to be worryingly high. These sweatshirts with built-in hoods had recently been targeted by the government as a symptom of yob culture, and their wearers were being excluded from shopping centres and public places.

I followed a group of pedestrians walking the same direction as me. One of them was wearing a hoodie. On the back it had a slogan. 'Save the...' Something. I couldn't quite make it out. But the protective sentiments sounded reassuring. At the zebra crossing, I caught up with the group, and could see the words more clearly, 'Save the Hoodie.' Nice.

Wrexham Road, a red brick cul-de-sac, looked like it had been created as part of a set for a gritty soap opera: mostly *East Enders*, but with a touch of *Coronation Street* and a nod to *On The Buses*. On one corner is London Transport's huge Bow bus garage. On the other corner was a shop so perfectly proportioned and stereotypical that it looked like a television props department had created it with just a little too much attention to detail for it to be real. Asian proprietors. Posters for Irn Bru. Signs for the National Lottery. Handwritten cards advertising ironing services and lost cats.

I walk down the road itself. It's tidy and well-kept. A two-bedroomed house here will cost you just under £300,000. Geezers in dark-blue London Transport jackets come and go; the street is used as overspill parking for the bus garage. I wonder what the name 'Wrexham' means to the workers here? A draw on the football pools, perhaps. Not much more.

Local history records hold few clues as to why the street got its name. It was one of a small number of streets of terraced houses laid out on part of the Grove Hall Estate in Bow, in around 1910. An entry in the minutes of the Poplar Borough Council (of which Bow then formed a part) in March 1907 says: "The London County Council has approved plans for laying out new streets on the Grove Hall Estate, Bow. Application has also been made for consent to the naming of such streets as follows: Wrexham Road. Baldock Street. Jebb Street. Ridgdale Street. Neve Street. Senlac Road. We see no objection to the names proposed, and have directed the London County Council be so informed." Was there some exiled Wrexhamite among the speculative builders, perhaps? It wasn't that there was some kind of Welsh theme, or even a town theme, going on. But here it is still, a century on, some corner of a foreign city that is forever Wales.

I reach the end of the cul-de-sac, a steep drop down to the thundering traffic of the Blackwall Tunnel Approach Road. Walking back on the other side, I pass a small close of new houses. 'BryMay Close'. The name scratches at my memory for a few moments before the recollection finally flares. 'BryMay' as in Bryant and May, the match company. It was on their matchboxes. Was the factory around here, then? I look up at the skyline. Sure enough, there's a giant, gaunt-windowed redbrick factory with a huge square tower like some kind of Victorian Protestant minaret.

Rounding the corner to get a closer view, I learn that this was indeed the famous match factory, once employing three thousand people, many of them young girls, in appalling conditions and for pitiful pay. It was the scene of the celebrated industrial action led by the radical campaigner Annie Besant, the Match Girls' Strike of 1888. She won.

The factory operated from 1861 to 1979. Whether its closure had something to do with the election of Mrs Thatcher's Conservative government that year, I don't know. But, thinking of how she destroyed the mining industry to punish the unions for the hard time they'd given a previous Tory government, I wouldn't put it past her to have carried out some belated revenge on behalf of the Victorian industrialists. Either way, these days, the factory is a gated community of seven hundred and thirty-three designer apartments, with uniformed African security guards manning the gatehouse. Both Mrs Thatcher and Annie Besant are history now.

Wrexham Road isn't the only street in London with a Wrexham connection. Taking a shortcut through Belgravia recently, I came across Minera Mews. Closer inspection showed that this did indeed have a traceable connection with the Wrexham area. It was next door to Chester Row, and a stroll down the Mews itself showed a plaque noting that the land belonged to Grosvenor Estates, the property empire of the Duke of Westminster, Gerald Grosvenor, whose home is at Eaton Hall near Chester and who has extensive land holdings in the area of Minera to the west of Wrexham. There, the name of the City Arms pub, named after the city of Chester, is evidence of the connection with the family of the Duke, who was, until 2004, the richest man in Britain, with a fortune of nearly seven billion pounds, derived largely from his ownership of large areas of the most expensive property in central London. A one-bedroom flat in Minera Mews will cost you no less than £800,000. You could buy the whole of Minera for that.

These are not the only places outside Wales which are named after Wrexham. There are Wrexham Roads in several towns bordering Wrexham, for obvious reasons. Less obvious is why there's a Wrexham Road in Slough. And further afield, why are there at least two Wrexham Roads in Australia? There's one in Windsor, Melbourne, Victoria, and the other near the town of Bulli in – of all the places to name after a north Wales town – New *South* Wales. In the United States, meanwhile, there are at least ten streets or roads similarly named. In Columbus, Ohio, you can walk down Wrexham Avenue to visit

Wrexham Park. You can walk down Wrexham Avenue in Massillon, Ohio too, and you have a choice of no fewer than four Wrexham Courts: in Tonwawanda, New York; Hampton, Virginia; Herndon, Virginia and Bensalem, Pennsylvania. There's a Wrexham Circle in Mechanicsville, Virginia, and Wrexham Drive in Snellville, Georgia. And, in Chesterfield, Virginia there's Old Wrexham Road. But  there's no record, sadly, of any *New* Wrexham Road.

Wilmington, Delaware, has its own Wrexham Road too. Wilmington, however, isn't the most obvious place to have one, unlike neighbouring Pennsylvania, the heartland of Welsh America, where Welsh emigrants have left their mark with placenames like Nantyglo, Cambria, Bala Cynwyd, and Bryn Mawr. In Pennsylvania, mailboxes marked 'Griffith', 'Jones' and 'Evans' sport red dragons, and cemeteries have gravestones where Welsh poetry is carved into the slate.

But Wilmington isn't like that. It's the centre of the Dupont industrial complex in the USA, and headquarters to some of the world's major banks. Recently, after doing a reading in nearby Delta in Pennsylvania, I was driven to Wilmington, to stay with family friends, Susan and Bill McClellan. Susan, my sister-in-law's sister, is originally from Buckley, only a few miles from Wrexham. She works as a shamanic practitioner, bringing spiritual enlightenment to her clients through Native American traditional practices. She's lived in America for around a quarter of a century, but in all that time, hadn't come across the street, only a few minutes from her house, named after her own home town.

When we visited, it was Columbus Day, a national holiday. The road was a comfortable residential street in a network of similar areas; with generously-proportioned bungalows, many with swimming pools, set in manicured lawns, with room for three or more cars on the drive. It was close to Hallowe'en, and the houses were decorated with pumpkins, scarecrows and plastic skulls dangling from trees. But it was as hot as a summer's day. The sound of cicadas in the bushes; the crunch of acorns underfoot; the call of a bird.

"A blue jay," says Susan.

"How do you know that?"

"It's one of my totem animals," she tells me, matter-of-factly.

It's quiet. Most people are away for the day. We pass one father and his children cleaning their car. Did they know how their street got its name? No, the father tells us. But he does have friends in England. None of the adjacent streets have names with any Welsh connection: Chinchilla Drive; Bandur Close; Northcrest Drive; Walter Drive; Zebley Road. The best guess I can make for a connection is that we're immediately next-door to Pennsylvania's Chester County.

Apart from the name, there's nothing to remind you of home. Not the cars: Windstar; Buick; Chevrolet; Chrysler New Yorker; Ford Taurus; pick-ups. Not the street furniture: mailboxes; *News Journal* vending stall; fire hydrant. Not the signs: the US flags; 'Elect Joe Biden to Congress'; 'Home of an Eagles Fan'; 'Northcrest Park, Closed dusk to dawn, No intoxicating beverages or drugs.' Definitely not like home.

That weekend, I accompanied Susan and Bill to Kirkridge Retreat Centre a few hours' drive away in northern Pennsylvania, for a shamanic get-together conducted by her mentor and now fellow-teacher, Tom Cowan.

I'd met Tom a couple of years before when he visited Wales, pursuing his interest in Celtic shamanism. As we drove from Aberystwyth up to Caernarfon, he asked me diffidently about Taliesin. "Ah, yes, the shapeshifter," I said, trying to sound as knowledgeable as I could, and putting together the little I knew about the shadowy figure of the ninth-century bard who is also a protean shaman who incarnates in different forms throughout the ages. Tom listened thoughtfully, nodded.

A few weeks afterwards, I read Tom's seminal book on Celtic shamanism, *Fire in the Head* – and learned more about Taliesin than I thought there was to know. I made a mental note that next time I ventured to discourse on Celtic myths, I'd check how much the questioner already knows about them. You live and learn.

I learned at Kirkridge too. Susan, her north-east-Wales accent untouched by her quarter century in the States, led the group in rituals adapted from Native American practices. Drums, blankets, rattles, stones, sage-scented incense, power animals, chakras, earth labyrinths, poetry, dream-journeys and vision-quests. The circle of seekers, native Americans if not Native Americans, listened, nodded, learned. Through the huge picture windows of the octagonal lounge at Kirkridge, the autumn woods of the Pocono range of the Appalachians were a sea of red and gold as far as the eye could see.

After the two days were over, we were driving back along the free-way to Wilmington in Susan's silver Range Rover Discovery. I said to her.

"Do you know what I was thinking when I was watching you there with your drum and your rattle and your circle of listeners?"

"No. What?"

"Well, I was just listening to the drum, and breathing in the sage smoke, and letting my mind wander..."

"And...?"

"And I was thinking, 'Susan, girl. You've come a hell of a long way from Buckley.'"

YALE

You have to travel more than a day's journey north of Wilmington to find the most prominent foreign location to bear the name Wrexham. It's at Yale University in New Haven, Connecticut, where a replica of the tower of Wrexham's St Giles' Church has dominated the skyline of Branford College since the early 1920s. There's even a brief shot of it at the beginning of *Raiders of the Lost Ark*, when the adventurer Indiana Jones is shown in his other life as an academic archaeologist. The Wrexham connection comes through Elihu Yale, Wrexham's most famous export. His epitaph, self-penned shortly before his death in 1721, and carved on his tomb which lies near the tower of St Giles' Church in Wrexham, gives a useful summary:

> Born in America, in Europe bred,
> In Africa travell'd and in Asia wed,
> Where long he liv'd and thriv'd; In London dead.
> Much good, some ill, he did; so hope all's even
> And that his soul thro' mercy's gone to Heaven.
> You that survive and read this tale, take care
> For this most certain exit to prepare.
> Where blest in peace, the actions of the just
> Smell sweet and blossom in the silent dust.

"So hope all's even". Elihu clearly had a businesslike approach to the question of his eternal destiny, and expected the Almighty to look at his life's balance sheet like a shrewd accountant. But after all, Elihu was a highly successful trader, so such an approach was only natural.

He was born in Boston, Massachusetts, in 1649, the son of David Yale whose gentry family were from Plas-yn-Iâl near Llanarmon-yn-Iâl, in the hills about nine miles west of Wrexham town. The name Yale comes from an anglicisation of Iâl. Elihu himself only spent the first four years of his life in America, being taken subsequently by his family to Britain, and later making his fortune as a trader and then governor in India, where he worked for the British East India Company.

He had a talent for leaving his mark. To this day, thanks to Elihu, the city of Chennai, formerly Madras, in the Tamil district of southern India, has a historic stronghold named after the patron saint of Wales. Elihu bought the fortification from the native princes in 1686, striking the deal for as much of the surrounding land as could be encompassed in a cannon shot from the fort. He made sure he had the mother of all cannons for the job, and, by firing shots in all directions, soon had a substantial tract of land under his control; the communities within its boundary are known to this day as 'cannonball villages', and the fort, in Elihu's tribute to his own Welsh roots, is called Fort St David. The fort was the refuge where Robert Clive, whose descendants subsequently became earls of Powis and who still live at the family seat near Welshpool, managed to maintain a British presence in India in the face of French competition. And it was from here that Clive later launched the British conquest of the subcontinent. The British Raj? Could never have happened without a Wrexham man.

However, Elihu didn't let national sentiment get in the way of advancement, and soon after acquiring Fort St David, he was made governor of Madras, and was based in Fort St *George*. It was here that he committed the 'ill' he mentioned on his gravestone. What kind of wrongdoing would one expect from a sharp businessman? Embezzlement maybe? False accounting? A bit of insider dealing? Yes, he did all that; he was sacked as governor after five years for neglect and for speculating with company funds. But it's his attitude to labour relations that was the real shocker. One day, Elihu's groom took his horse without his master's permission and rode it for three days. The excursion was, apparently, intended to be for the good of the groom's health. It had the opposite effect. Elihu had the groom arrested and demanded that he be executed. When his lawyers told him that going AWOL wasn't a capital offence, he promptly had the charge changed to piracy and had the man hanged. The case caused outrage, and when Elihu returned to England in 1699, together with five tons of spices, jewels and leather goods (costing £24,000 in customs duty), he was tried for abuse of the judicial process, but managed to escape with a penalty rather than jail or worse.

Perhaps there was some desire to make amends when, nearly twenty years later, in 1718, Elihu, by that time one of Europe's richest men, and a noted benefactor of the arts, was approached by Jeremiah Dummer, the colonial agent for Massachusetts and Connecticut, who was collecting donations to set up the Collegiate College at New

Haven. "The business of good men is to spread religion and learning among mankind..." he told Elihu, who responded in 1718 by donating nine bales of goods, four hundred and seventeen books and a portrait of King George I. The bales sold for £562, a huge sum in its day, and the books sold for £600. Together these made the biggest gift the college received before 1837. It was enough to ensure him earthly immortality as the new institution duly named itself after its largest benefactor.

According to *American Heritage* magazine, Elihu Yale is really 'the most overrated philanthropist' in American history. The magazine argued that the tireless fundraiser Jeremiah Dummer was really more deserving of the honour. However, the magazine went on to point out, the college trustees had not wanted to name their new institution 'Dummer College'. Its alumni would then have been 'Dummies' instead of 'Yalies'. Yale it was, and no-one's changing it now.

In 1999, though, there was a serious attempt to change a name in Wrexham to suit the image of Yale University. For most Wrexham people, the name 'Yale' means just one thing – the local sixth-form, now tertiary, college. It's my own *alma mater*, (class of 1980) and I was some years into university life in England before I learned not to make casual references to 'when I was at Yale' to people for whom the only Yale was on the other side of the Atlantic. However, apart from such occasional mild confusion, quickly explained, there seemed little reason why the American academic giant and its humble Welsh namesake couldn't co-exist happily, as they had done since the Wrexham college was founded in the 1920s.

The internet changed all that. In the late 1990's, college authorities in New Haven, browsing the still-infant world wide web, were shocked to find another institution calling itself 'Yale College'. Their response followed the time-honoured American approach to conflict-resolution. They sued. The mild-mannered response of the Wrexham college was that students were hardly likely to mistake a local-authority sixth-form college in a provincial Welsh town (courses up to A-level and NVQ, including Hairdressing and Beauty Therapy, and Food Hygeine) for one of the world's most prestigious centres of learning (courses up to post-doctoral including Near Eastern Languages and Civilizations, Hellenic Studies, and Cellular and Molecular Physiology). New Haven weren't prepared to take that risk, and the Wrexham college was forced to specify its name as 'Yale College of Wrexham, Wales.' As one newspaper headline at the time said: 'There's Gratitude'. But, on reflection, as a compromise, it was acceptable. And Wrexham's used to compromises. It has to be. After all, more than anything, this is a border town.

THE PHOTOGRAPHS

THANKS AND ACKNOWLEDGEMENTS

In writing *Real Wrexham,* I have had the benefit of help from many sources, past and present Firstly, *diolch yn fawr* to my parents, Oswald and Eunice Davies for love, support, advice and practical help. I am grateful to those who took their time to share their areas of expertise with me during my research visits: Dave Cooke; Peter Appleton and Jason Parry; Elin Llwyd Morgan; Susan and Bill McClellan; Malcolm Hughes; Alan Owens; Terry Heath; Rhys Wynne; Tom Ellis; Derrick Pratt and the late Leslie Kynaston. Many people, in Wales, the UK and abroad, were ready to help with advice, contacts and information: Nick Bourne at the BBC's North East Wales *Where I Live* website; Ena Woolford; Gary Pritchard; Anthony Brockway; Will Vaus; Joan Lewis Murphy; Silas D. McCaslin; Hedd ap Emlyn; Aled Lewis Evans; Lawrence Hourahane; Cochion Caerdydd and Malcolm Barr-Hamilton, borough archivist, Tower Hamlets Local History Library and Archives.

In terms of research sources, I have relied heavily on W. Alister Williams' comprehensive *The Encyclopaedia of Wrexham* for details and information; I have acknowledged specific instances in endnotes or in the text, and I am glad to record here my debt to this invaluable reference work. Thanks also to the anonymous creators and maintainers of Wrexham County Borough Council's exemplary website, which has been the source of much information. Any errors or omissions are entirely my responsibility. I am grateful to Peter Finch for his editorial guidance and vision with the project, and to the staff at Seren for their customary hard work. Thanks to my wife Sally, and my daughters Haf and Alaw for their patience and support. Finally, I dedicate this work to the people of Coedpoeth, the village where I had the privilege to be born and raised.

INDEX

THE AUTHOR

Grahame Davies was born in Coedpoeth in 1964. He was educated at the village's Penygelli and Ysgol Bryn Tabor schools, at Ysgol Morgan Llwyd and Yale Sixth Form College, at Anglia Ruskin University in Cambridge, where he gained a degree in English literature, and at Cardiff University, where he was awarded a doctorate. A poet, novelist, editor, literary critic and journalist, he is the author of more than a dozen books, including: *Cadwyni Rhyddid,* which won the 2002 Wales Book of the Year Prize; *The Chosen People,* a history of the Welsh relationship with the Jewish people, and *Everything Must Change,* which was described as 'the first post-national novel' in Wales. His work has been translated into many languages, and he travels worldwide as a poet and lecturer. He has lived in south Wales for over twenty years, but keeps close contact with the Wrexham area.